# THREE DISCOURSES
# ON IMAGINED OCCASIONS

KIERKEGAARD'S WRITINGS, X

# THREE DISCOURSES
# ON IMAGINED OCCASIONS

by Søren Kierkegaard

*Edited and Translated*
*with Introduction and Notes by*

Howard V. Hong and
Edna H. Hong

PRINCETON UNIVERSITY PRESS
PRINCETON, NEW JERSEY

*Library of Congress Cataloging-in-Publication Data*

*Kierkegaard, Søren, 1813–1855.*
*[Tre taler ved tænkte leiligheder. English]*
*Three discourses on imagined occasions / by Søren Kierkegaard ;*
*edited and translated with introduction and notes by Howard V. Hong*
*and Edna H. Hong*
*p. cm. — (Kierkegaard's writings; 10)*
*Translation of: Tre taler ved tænkte leiligheder.*
*Includes bibliographical references and index.*
*ISBN 0-691-03300-5 (cl)*
*1. Christian life—Lutheran authors. 2. God—Worship and love.*
*3. Marriage—Religious aspects—Christianity. 4. Death—Religious*
*aspects—Christianity. I. Hong, Howard Vincent, 1912– .*
*II. Hong, Edna Hatlestad, 1913– . III. Title. IV. Series:*
*Kierkegaard, Søren, 1813–1855. Works. English. 1978; 10.*
*BV4505.K48413 1993*
*248.4'841—dc20 92-36382*

*Preparation of this volume has been made possible in part by a grant from*
*the Division of Research Programs of the National Endowment*
*for the Humanities, an independent federal agency*

*Designed by Frank Mahood*

*Printed in the United States of America*

*1 3 5 7 9 10 8 6 4 2*

# CONTENTS

# HISTORICAL INTRODUCTION

*Three Discourses on Imagined Occasions* was the last of Kierkegaard's discourses in the series of signed works parallel to the first pseudonymous series, which culminated in what he at the time regarded as his final work, *Concluding Unscientific Postscript to* Philosophical Fragments, with an appended acknowledgment of the pseudonymous writings. The publication dates of the various discourses were always close to the dates of the pseudonymous works, in one instance (*Three Upbuilding Discourses* and *Repetition*) on the same day, and *Three Discourses on Imagined Occasions* was followed the next day by *Stages on Life's Way*.

| Pseudonymous | | Signed | |
|---|---|---|---|
| | **1843** | | **1843** |
| Feb. 20 | *Either/Or*, I-II ed. Victor Eremita | | |
| | | May 16 | *Two Upbuilding Discourses* |
| Oct. 16 | *Repetition* by Constantin Constantius | Oct. 16 | *Three Upbuilding Discourses* |
| Oct. 16 | *Fear and Trembling* by Johannes de Silentio | | |
| | | Dec. 6 | *Four Upbuilding Discourses* |
| | **1844** | | **1844** |
| | | March 5 | *Two Upbuilding Discourses* |
| | | June 8 | *Three Upbuilding Discourses* |

| | | | |
|---|---|---|---|
| June 13 | *Philosophical Fragments* by Johannes Climacus ed. S. Kierkegaard | | |
| June 17 | *The Concept of Anxiety* by Vigilius Haufniensis | | |
| June 17 | *Prefaces* by Nicolaus Notabene | | |
| | | Aug. 31 | *Four Upbuilding Discourses* |
| | 1845 | | 1845 |
| | | April 29 | *Three Discourses on Imagined Occasions* |
| April 30 | *Stages on Life's Way* pub. by Hilarius Bookbinder | | |
| May 19–20 | "A Cursory Observation Concerning a Detail in *Don Giovanni*" by Inter et Inter | | |

1846                                    1846
Feb. 27 *Concluding Unscientific Postscript*
by Johannes Climacus, with the appended
"A First and Last Explanation"
by S. Kierkegaard

In the latter half of 1844, while he was finishing the writing of *Stages*,[1] Kierkegaard worked also on a volume of six discourses on imagined occasions,[2] as well as on a "new science," "the Christian art of speaking, to be constructed *ad modum* [in the

---

[1] The instructions to the printer are dated "January 1845." See *Pap.* VI B 8:2.

[2] See Supplement, p. 126 (*Pap.* VI B 138).

manner of] Aristotle's *Rhetoric*."[3] This work, however, was laid aside temporarily because it would be "too discursive to serve as a kind of introduction to my few discourses."[4] His thinking on the subject took preliminary form in a piece[5] by Johannes de Silentio (pseudonymous author of *Fear and Trembling*) to serve as a preface to the discourses currently in preparation. How tentative this plan was is apparent in the stipulation that Silentio's preface was "not to be bound into the volume."[6]

Kierkegaard had the seeds of more than six discourses in mind. Among them were a discourse on death,[7] three on Peter's denial of Christ,[8] three on the Canaanite woman,[9] and two on suffering as guilty or innocent,[10] as well as funeral addresses for the king's deceased valet[11] and for the prophetess Anna.[12] Eventually the multitude was reduced to the three[13] that constitute the present volume of occasional discourses.

"Occasional" obviously does not mean "occurring now and then" but refers to an occasion as a specific event and situation. Johannes de Silentio, in the proposed preface to the occasional discourses, asserts: "In actual occasional discourses some things cannot very well be said because of the presence of the specific persons before one. Therefore the reverse is done here: the stated individualities are created by the discourse"[14]—hence the imagined occasions. This view is later echoed and amplified in the preface to *Upbuilding Discourses in Various Spirits*, of which Part One is "On the Occasion of a Confession":

[3] See Supplement, p. 110 (*Pap.* VI A 17) and pp. 110–11 (*Pap.* VI A 1, 18–19, 33).

[4] See Supplement, p. 112 (*Pap.* VI B 132).

[5] See Supplement, pp. 117–25 (*Pap.* VI B 128–31, 133).

[6] See Supplement, pp. 117–18, 119–25 (*Pap.* VI B 128, 133).

[7] See Supplement, pp. 109 (*Pap.* V A 36).

[8] See Supplement, pp. 114–15 (*Pap.* VI B 166, 168).

[9] See Supplement, p. 115 (*Pap.* VI B 167).

[10] See Supplement, p. 115–16 (*Pap.* VI B 169–70).

[11] See Supplement, p. 112 (*Pap.* VI B 149).

[12] See Supplement, p. 113 (*Pap.* VI B 153).

[13] See Supplement, pp. 126, 127 (*Pap.* VI B 100, 125:1).

[14] See Supplement, pp. 117–18 (*Pap.* VI B 128).

Although this little book (it can be called an occasional discourse, yet without having the occasion that creates the speaker and makes him an *authority* or the occasion that creates the reader and makes him a *learner*) in the situation of *actuality* is like a fancy, a dream in the daytime, yet it is not without confidence and not without hope of fulfillment. It seeks that single individual, to whom it gives itself wholly, by whom it wishes to be received as if it had arisen in his own heart, that single individual whom I with joy and gratitude call *my* reader, that single individual who willingly reads slowly, reads repeatedly, and who reads aloud—for his own sake. If it finds him, then in the remoteness of separation the understanding is complete when he keeps the book and the understanding to himself in the inwardness of appropriation.[15]

*Discourses on Imagined Occasions* was not only chronologically the companion piece to *Stages* but is also its counterpoise in content. "On the Occasion of a Confession," with an emphasis on stillness, wonder, and seeking God, is Kierkegaard's counterpoint to "*In Vino Veritas*" in *Stages*, with its banquet and speechmaking on erotic love.[16] "On the Occasion of a Wedding" deepens and rectifies Judge William's panegyric on marriage in *Either/Or*, II, and in the second part of *Stages*. And "At a Graveside," on the earnestness in life evoked by the earnest thought of death, constitutes an unambiguous sharpening of the implicit ethical and religious earnestness in Quidam's "'Guilty'/'Not Guilty'" in Part Three of *Stages*. One is perhaps justified in imagining that Kierkegaard alternated between his ordinary desk, spread with the ongoing manuscript of *Stages*, and his high desk at which he intermittently worked on *Discourses on Imagined Occasions*.

*Discourses on Imagined Occasions* is thematically related to other earlier and later works. The substance of "On the Occasion of a Confession" is extended in detail in Part One, on purity of heart, of *Discourses in Various Spirits* (1847), "An Oc-

---

15 *Upbuilding Discourses in Various Spirits*, p. 5, *KW* XV (*SV* VIII 117).
16 See *Stages on Life's Way*, pp. 7–86, *KW* XI (*SV* VI 13–83).

acquaintances, Victor Eremita and Constantinus [*sic*] Constantius, in the company of Johannes the Seducer, a fashion designer, and a young man whom the author as yet has not named. Over brimming glasses, they discuss the old question of the significance of woman but do not arrive at the same conclusion as the poet who declared her to be the Creator's most perfect masterpiece; one of them even declares fashion to be a woman because of its nonsensical fickleness that knows no other consistency than to become more and more starkly mad. The next section contains a piece by Judge William (also an acquaintance from *Either/Or*), in which he furnishes new contributions to the proper conception of marriage. The third section contains a tale of woe or, rather, the story of an engagement in the author's well-known style. If we have any negative criticism of these works, it is that the author seems to us to take almost too much time elaborating his reflections, with the result that they sometimes become somewhat prolix; however, we do thank him for the pleasure he has given us through these fine books, and we are happy that he will let us hear from him again soon.[24]

The rumor broadcast by Nathanson was confirmed very soon by "A First and Last Explanation," which was appended to *Concluding Unscientific Postscript*[25] (February 27, 1846); and his wish to hear from Magister Kierkegaard was copiously fulfilled not only by *Postscript* but by the "second authorship" (after the *Corsair* affair[26]), which was already under way by the time *Postscript* appeared.

[24] *Berlingske Tidende*, 108, May 6, 1845, col. 3–4. See *Stages*, pp. 646–51 (*Pap.* VI B 184) for Kierkegaard's unpublished response.

[25] See *Concluding Unscientific Postscript to* Philosophical Fragments, pp. [625–30], *KW* XII.1 (*SV* VII [545–49]).

[26] See Historical Introduction, *The* Corsair *Affair and Articles Related to the Writings*, pp. vii-xxxiii, *KW* XIII.

# THREE DISCOURSES
# ON IMAGINED OCCASIONS

by Søren Kierkegaard

casional Discourse."[17] "On the Occasion of a Wedding" is not only a companion piece to Judge William's piece in *Stages* but also to "The Esthetic Validity of Marriage" in *Either/Or*, II[18] (1843). The theme of "At a Graveside" appears *passim* in *Eighteen Discourses*[19] (1843–1844) and in Chapter IX of *Works of Love*[20] (1847) on recollecting one who is dead.

*Three Discourses on Imagined Occasions* was presumably printed in the usual edition of 525 copies, of which 181 had been sold by July 1847, two years after its publication.[21] Kierkegaard was his own publisher, as he had been for fifteen volumes and continued to be for four more.[22] A second edition was published in 1875. In 1855, the year Kierkegaard died, the remaining sheets of *Three Discourses on Imagined Occasions* were included by Reitzel in a composite volume under the title *Gudelige Taler*,[23] a companion volume to the composite volume *Atten opbyggelige Taler*, which was an assemblage of the six small volumes of discourses from 1843 and 1844. During Kierkegaard's lifetime, all of his signed discourses were remaindered and were gathered in two composite volumes of exceeding rarity.

The scant reception *Discourses on Imagined Occasions* received from Kierkegaard's contemporaries was commensurate with the paucity and brevity of the reviews. There was one, signed "-n." (Mendel Levin Nathanson, editor of *Berlingske Tidende*). It was not, however, so much a review as an announcement of publication, also of *Stages*, and the first publicizing of a rumor

[17] Pp. 3–154, *KW* XV (*SV* VIII 115–242).

[18] Pp. 3–154, *KW* IV (*SV* II 3–140).

[19] See, for example, pp. 79, 181–86, 272, 280, 288–89, 350–51, 385, *KW* V (*SV* III 296; IV 75–80, 155–56, 161–62, 168–70; V 127, 156).

[20] *KW* XVI (*SV* IX 327–29).

[21] See Frithiof Brandt and Else Rammel, *Søren Kierkegaard og Pengene* (Copenhagen: Levin & Munksgaard, 1935), p. 18.

[22] See ibid., pp. 13, 31.

[23] The volume also included *The Lily in the Field and the Bird of the Air, Three Discourses at the Communion on Fridays, An Upbuilding Discourse, Two Discourses at the Communion on Fridays,* and *The Changelessness of God.*

couched in the language of appreciation mingled with critical advice.

**Literature.** Mag. Kierkegaard: *Three Discourses*; *Stages of Life*. It is well known that the hero in the old oriental fairy tales usually has some magic means to make his wishes come true in the real world. One would think that Mag. Kierkegaard possessed a kind of magic wand by which he instantaneously conjures up his books, so incredible has his literary activity been in recent years, if we dare believe the rumor that presumably is correct in claiming him to be the author of *Either/Or* and the series of books that apparently comes from the same hand. Productivity of that kind is not always a clear recommendation, since very often it signifies hasty, superficial work, but this is so far from being the case here that, on the contrary, each of these works is remarkable for a depth of thought that pursues its object to its most minute thread and in addition unfolds a rare beauty and elegance of language, and particularly a fluency that surpasses that of any contemporary Danish writer. When we consider also that an authentic poetic genius is manifest in many places, we cannot refrain from wishing that the author would also venture in directions other than the philosophical hypothesizing that until now has been dominant in his writings. The *Three Discourses on Imagined Occasions*, which he has recently presented to us, are entirely in the same spiritual family as the author's earlier published discourses and are marked by the same beauty of form and richness of content. The discourses are a confessional sermon, a wedding ceremony, and a graveside meditation; in the first one he tells what it means to seek God, in the second he develops the beautiful theme that love in marriage will overcome everything, and, finally, in the third discourse he poignantly portrays death's culmination as the final end of our earthly existence. *Life's Stages*, a collection of three longer sections, which a "Mr. Hilarius Bookbinder has had the kindness to have published," reminds us not a little of *Either/Or*. In the first section, entitled "*In Vino Veritas*," we meet our earlier

DEDICATED TO THE MEMORY OF

MY LATE FATHER

# Michael Pedersen Kierkegaard

Although this little book (occasional discourses, as it could be called, notwithstanding that it does not have the occasion that makes the speaker and makes him an *authority* or the occasion that makes the reader and makes him a *learner*) is entirely unsolicited and thus in its deficiency entirely unjustified, is entirely without the support of the circumstances and thus without assistance in its full development, yet it is not without hope and above all not without bold confidence. It seeks that single individual whom I with joy and gratitude call *my* reader, or it does not even seek him. Unaware of the time and the hour, it quietly waits for that right reader to come like the bridegroom and to bring the occasion along with him. Let each do a share— the reader therefore more. The meaning lies in the appropriation. Hence the *book*'s joyous *giving of itself.* Here there are no worldly "mine" and "thine" that separate and prohibit appropriating what is the neighbor's. Admiration is in part really envy and thus a misunderstanding; and criticism, for all its justification, is in part really opposition and thus a misunderstanding; and recognition in a mirror is only a fleeting acquaintance and thus a misunderstanding—but to see correctly and not want to forget what the mirror is incapable of effecting, that is the appropriation, and the appropriation is the *reader's* even greater, is his triumphant *giving of himself.*

*S. K.*

# On the Occasion of a Confession[1]

²FATHER in heaven, how well we know that seeking always has its promise; how much the more, then, seeking you, the giver of all the promises and of all good gifts! How well we know that the seeker does not always need to wander out into the world, because the more holy that is which he seeks, the closer it is to him, and if he seeks you, O God, you are closest of all to him! But we also know that seeking always has its toil and its spiritual trial—how much more, then, the terror in seeking you, you Mighty One! If even the person who
in thought puts his trust in his kinship, if even he with his
thought does not without terror venture out into those decisions when he through doubt seeks your footprint in the wise
order of existence, when he through despair seeks your footprint in the obedience of rebellious events to a providence; if he
whom you called your friend, the one who walks in your sight,
if even he does not without trembling seek friendship's en-
counter with you, you the only Mighty One; if the one praying, who loves you with his whole heart, if even he does not
without anxiety venture into prayer's struggle with his God; if
even the one dying, for whom you exchange life, if even he
does not without shuddering relinquish the temporal when
you call; if even the wretched one whom the world gives sheer
suffering, if even he, too, does not without terror flee to you,
you who do not soothe a little but are everything—how, then,
does the sinner dare to seek you, you righteous God! But that is
why he does not seek you as these do, but he seeks you in the
confession of sins.

³There is indeed a place for that, my listener, and you know
where; and there is indeed an opportunity for it, my listener,
and you know how; and there is indeed a moment, and it is
called this very day. How still! In God's house there is peace
[*Fred*], but deepest within the inclosure [*det Omfredede*] there is a
closed room. The one who goes there seeks stillness; the one
who sits there is in stillness; even if there is speaking, the stillness only intensifies. How still! There is no fellowship—each
one is by himself; there is no call for united effort—each one is

V
177

V
178

called to individual responsibility; there is no invitation to community—each one is alone. The person who is making a confession is alone—indeed, as alone as a dying person. Whether those who were precious and dear to him and who love him are crowded in great numbers around the bed of the dying one, or whether he lies there abandoned by the world because he abandoned it or it abandoned him—the dying one is alone, they are both struggling alone. The mind strays, and thousands, ten thousands, do not restrain it if the solitary one does not know comfort.

Whether thousands were waiting and yearning for the one who in confessing seeks stillness, or whether the one leaving confession is the insignificant and wretched person no one waits for and no one troubles about, this difference is only a jest; the truth is, the earnest truth was, that they both were alone. All his friends, the world's glory, and the far-flung importance of his achievements are of no help to the powerful person—unless it would be to disturb the stillness for him, which is the greatest harm. It does not harm the poor nobody to be abandoned if it helps him to find stillness. It is difficult for a camel to go through the eye of a needle[4] and difficult for the man of the world to find stillness; whether he is powerful or insignificant, it is difficult to find stillness in life's noise, difficult to find it where it is even when he himself does not bring the noise along with him.

How still and how earnest! Yet there is no one who accuses; who would dare to be the accuser where everyone is guilty. Yet there is no one who judges; who would dare to judge where everyone considers his own accounting. There is no one who accuses except one's thoughts, no one who judges except the one who sees into what is hidden[5] and hears confessions in secret. Yes, even when there is speaking, you are indeed the one who is speaking with yourself through the speaker's voice. What the speaker will say just to you, only you know; how you understand his words, he does not know—only you know that. Even if the speaker were your best friend, he still cannot know it as you know it. If you do not listen in this way, then you are not listening properly, then what he says is a noise that disturbs the stillness, and your attentiveness is a diversion that violates the stillness.

Whoever is afraid of this stillness, let him avoid it, but he does not dare to deny that it exists, because he does fear it. Whoever[6] says that he sought stillness but did not find it is an envious deceiver who wants to frustrate others, because otherwise he would be silent and sad or he would say, "I did not seek it properly; therefore I did not find it." Nothing, nothing in the whole world, even if an earthquake shook the pillars of the church, not the most erroneous words of the most foolish of people, not the foulness of the basest hypocrite, can take the stillness away from you, but something very minor can certainly give someone the occasion to seek a false pretext. No, nothing except you yourself can take it away from you; just as little as all the world's power and all its wisdom and the united efforts of all humanity can give it to you, just as little can you yourself take it and give it away. It cannot be obtained for nothing, but it cannot be bought with gold; it cannot be taken by violence, but it does not come as a dream when you are sleeping; it does not haggle about terms, even if you wanted to benefit the whole human race. If you give everything away, that still does not necessarily mean that it is gained, but if you gain it you can then gladly possess everything as one who has nothing.[7]

Whoever says that this stillness does not exist is merely making noise. Have you ever really heard that anyone in stillness made up his mind that it does not exist, even though you probably have heard big words and loud talk and noisy doings to get rid of stillness in order to have, instead of conscience and stillness and God's voice delivering judgment in stillness, a nature-echo from the crowd, a confused collective scream, a general opinion in which one, out of cowardice, fearing for oneself, is not alone. But you, my listener, if you fear this stillness, even though you are doing your best to have a conscience (without stillness conscience does not exist at all) and to have a good conscience, then keep on, then endure it; this

V
179

stillness is not the stillness of death in which you perish, it is not the sickness unto death[8]—it is the transition to life.

[9]So, then, the confessor seeks God in the confession of sins, and the confession is the road and is a biding place[10] on the road of salvation, where one pauses and collects one's thoughts and makes an accounting. And is it not true and proper that an accounting should be without deceit—then there is stillness, then everyone's mouth is stopped,[11] then everyone becomes guilty and cannot answer once in a thousand times.[12] With the help of distraction one becomes less guilty, perhaps even justified. But what lamentable justification! It is not unjust for you to forgive another person for his sake if he asks your forgiveness, or if you believe that he wishes it for God's sake, who requires it, or for your own sake, so you may not be disturbed. You are not accepting a bribe because you heed the prompting to reconciliation within you; neither are you procrastinating along the way if you, although you are the injured party, seek peace with your adversary while he is still on the way.[13] Neither are you defrauding God of what belongs to him if you sell forgiveness for nothing; you are not wasting your time or misusing it if you ponder what may well serve as an excuse; and if no excuse is to be found you are not deceived if you, by means of love's holy deceit that transforms all the world's ridicule of your weakness into heavenly joy over your victory, believe that the offense must be excusable. But when it is a matter of your own accounting, then you certainly would do wrong to forgive yourself the least little thing, because one's own righteousness is even worse than one's own blackest private guilt. Then you would indeed be accepting a bribe if you followed the promptings of irresponsibility and craftiness in your own affairs; then you would be hindering yourself along the road and hindering the fervor of the spirit; then you would be wasting your time and misusing it in looking for escapes—indeed, then you would be deceived by a blasphemous deception, deceived precisely when you found the excuse!

Yes, alas, it is a strange transition, a change that makes the head swim! One moment ago the same person was going

along, rich and powerful, and now, a moment later, although
nothing has happened in the meantime, he cannot answer once
in a thousand times. Who indeed is the rich and powerful one to
whom the discourse refers here, who else but the injured party,
the oppressed one, the one who has been treated unfairly, the
one violated! Perhaps the perpetrator of violence who tramples
on the oppressed, perhaps the powerful one whose path is
marked by the wrongs he does, perhaps the rich whose wealth
was increased by widows' tears, perhaps the despairing person
who violates and mocks—perhaps all of these people cared but
little about forgiveness; yet surely no king who rules over king-
doms and countries, no Croesus who possesses everything,
and no philanthropist who feeds the hungry possesses anything as great or has anything as great to give away or anything
as needful to give away as the person whose forgiveness someone else needs. Needs—indeed, needs it as the primary necessity. If anyone does not think so, it is still needed just as much—
and the injured party possesses the most. [14]A pagan whose
name is inseparable from the idea of conquests and power said
when his enemy showed the highest courage (so it seemed,
alas, to the pagans) by committing suicide, "There he robbed
me of my most glorious victory, because I would have forgiven
him."[15] Someone else said, "Because I love much, I will not ask
for forgiveness. My wrong is perhaps not very great, forgiveness surely a very small thing to ask, but if it is not obtained,
then the wrong is infinite and the power of forgiveness an
infinite superiority over me."[16] So, then, the innocent injured
party was the rich man. But a moment ago in the setting of the
world he dared to say, "Go ahead and do an injustice to me; you
will still lose the most, because you need my forgiveness"—
and now a moment later the stillness encompasses him; he does
not know what he has to forgive, and the accounting shows
that he cannot answer once in a thousand times. This is how the
accounting is if he has the stillness around him and does not
himself bring along the disturbance. The accounting of the
person who did the wrong is the same as that of the person who
was purest of all, even that of the innocent injured party. For

V
181

this reason someone may be afraid of this stillness and its power and the infinite nothing into which it plunges all dissimilarities, even those of wrongs and forgiveness, and of the abyss into which the solitary one sinks in stillness.

It is the same as when the person who renounces the world shudders at the emptiness that seems to manifest itself. But one moment ago he desired so much and aspired and strove and slept badly at night and asked the latest news about others and envied some and ignored others and was unobtrusive in the right place and was active in friendship and enmity and forecast the weather and knew which way the wind was blowing and changed his plans and strove again and won and lost and never grew weary and kept his eye on the reward and caught a glimpse of the profits—and now, yes, the poor deceived man!—if in this renunciation he did not find the one thing needful, the poor deceived man who deceived himself, the poor man who by his own act became the victim of life's derision, because now the great thing he desired was perhaps realized, now he became rich, right now, oh, what despair, why right now, why not yesterday, but now when he did not entirely desire but also did not entirely renounce it!

It is the same with the person who experienced that there is a stillness in which every human being becomes guilty and only learned to fear it. If he was regarded as righteous in the eyes of people, and this was what he craved, if he was the injured party but was defiantly in proud possession of forgiveness, if he was not without guilt but enjoyed some esteem in the world—alas, the poor deceived man, how indignant he must be with the person who led him into and then led him astray in that stillness—but no one can do that, and his anger is powerless. Poor deceived man, if he were given the citizens' crown of justice by the public, an accolade he coveted; if thousands agreed to call him the man of justice in the nation, something his conceited ears delighted to hear—why now, now when his ears are probably not entirely stopped up, but he has not entirely comprehended the infinite secret of stillness either! Poor deceived man, if the guilty party now came to his door, if the moment when forgiveness could be dearly purchased was there, the moment of triumph he had joyfully anticipated, why now, why not yesterday, why now, now when he indeed did not voluptuously relish the vehemence of revenge and pride, but he did not entirely comprehend the earnest message of his own guilt either! The person who comprehended this was truly not deceived. Blessed is the one who understands this. If anyone has the task of preaching, of teaching others about their guilt, of teaching—something that this discourse, which is without authority, does not do—he does have the consolation that the purest of heart is precisely the one most willing to comprehend his own guilt most deeply. When it is a matter of that greatest and most daring venture of placing everyone under guilt when one is guilty oneself, there where even the brave one's thought comes to a standstill if he does not fear to include himself, but thought offers opposition at the sight of what, humanly speaking, is pure and lovable, at the sight of the beautiful purity of young womanhood that is ignorant of the world, unfamiliar with its incitements, and is sincerely meek and humble—there, if the task of the discourse bids him proclaim sin as the common lot of the human race, there he will find an understanding that perhaps humiliates him himself.

The confessor seeks God in the confession of sins, and the confession is the road and is a biding place on the road of salvation, where one pauses and collects one's thoughts. We shall, then, pause and on the occasion of a confession speak about:

### what it means to seek God.

And we shall define it more precisely by bearing in mind that without purity no human being can see God and without becoming a sinner no human being can come to know him.

If anyone feels made to pause in a wrong way at the task, then let him throw away the discourse lest the person who runs faster be detained by the slow one. The value of a meditation is, of course, always dubious; at times it can help one come to what is crucial, and at times it can also hinder—just as a short preliminary run can be of help at the crucial point of a jump but a preliminary run of several miles would even prevent it. But if

V
183

anyone has frequently felt made to pause in life without, however, finding stillness, if he has sought stillness where it indeed
is and yet has not really found it and reproaches himself for it, if
he has fought and yet not won, then let him try again, let him
move along with the discourse, but freely and voluntarily.
There is nothing that binds him, no obligation; no reproach
awaits him if he fails, inasmuch as the discourse is indeed without authority. But neither would he want the discourse to say
of the stillness in that solemn and sacred place that it is of such a
nature that if a person could remain there and did not have to go
out into life's confusion again he would then always have the
stillness with him, because the person who demands that demands too much of the discourse, namely, that it should deceive him, as if it were the place, externally understood, that
determined the outcome, as if the very same thing would not
happen to him if he remained in that solemn and sacred place as
happens to him in the world, as if he would not then first and
foremost be terrified by an illusion in which he had been reas-
sured that it was the place that counted. To be sure, a poet has
rightly said that a sigh to God without words is the best worship;[17] then one could also believe that the infrequent visit to
the sacred place, when one comes from far away, would be the
best worship, because both contribute to the illusion. A sigh
without words is the best worship if the thought of God is only
to shed a twilight glow over existence, like the blue mountains
on the distant horizon, if the unclarity of the soul's condition is
to be satisfied with the greatest possible ambiguity. But if God
is to be present to the soul, then the sigh presumably finds the
thought, and the thought presumably the words—but also the
difficulty, of which one has no inkling at a distance. In our day
we are told to the point of fatuousness that it is not the highest
to live in stillness, where there is no danger—to the point of
fatuousness, because danger is there just as much as in confusion, and, to come to the point, the great thing is neither to be
in the solitude nor to be in the confusion, but the great thing is
to overcome the danger—and the most mediocre thing is to
work oneself weary pondering which is the more difficult,
because that kind of work is futile and neither here nor there,

like the worker himself, who, after all, is neither in the confusion nor in the solitude but in the busy absentmindedness of thoughts.

If, finally, anyone on account of his many enterprises and busy work thinks that he does not have time to read this kind of discourse—well, he may be entirely right in thinking that he has no time to read this discourse, which gladly waits to the last for consideration; but if that means that he has no time at all to be concerned about what is the concern of the discourse, that stillness, then the discourse, even if the busy person found amid his many enterprises a free time for making a hasty protest, the discourse will not make itself ridiculous by responding to it. The many enterprises are perhaps of dubious merit; perhaps they may also become fewer for him if he considers that stillness, and the many enterprises will above all be perceived to be one more reason for more frequently seeking the stillness of the accounting, in which one does not reckon with dollars and cents or with distinctions and debasements and other imagined quantities.

If the seeker is seeking something outside himself as something external, as something not under his control, then what is sought is in a specific place. If he merely finds the place where it is—well, then he is helped, then he grasps it and his seeking is at an end. In the same manner everyone once knew at an early age that many beautiful things existed but did not definitely know the place. Alas, even if many have forgotten this childhood knowledge, have all in that way become truly wiser, including the one who instead of the unity of that beautiful fullness has won the duplexity of doubt and the halfheartedness of resolution!

If the seeker is assumed to be unable to do anything himself to find the place, he thinks wishfully. Everyone was once like that in early youth. Alas, even if many have changed, have all therefore also truly changed for the better, also the one who instead of the uncertain wealth of the wish won the certain misery of mediocrity!

When the person wishing sees his wish fulfilled, he wonders,

V
184

just as by wishing he already was in the state of wonder. Everyone was once like that in his early youth—not, as is unjustly said of youth, good to lure into foolish endeavors, but inwardly good to lure into the unqualified blessed giving of oneself to wonder, the honest gratuity that the wishing person faithfully saves for the moment of fulfillment. Alas, even if many have lost this haste in wanting to give like for like, just as he also has learned to disparage the wish, is this haggling therefore honesty that does not really wish and does not really wonder and thus gives like for like, is this honesty therefore a gain! —The person who wishes also seeks, but his seeking is in the dark, not so much in regard to the object of the wish as in regard to his not knowing whether he is getting closer to it or further away.

V
185

Among the many goods there is one that is the highest, that is not defined by its relation to the other goods, because it is the highest, and yet the person wishing does not have a definite idea of it, because it is the highest as the unknown[18]—and this good is God. The other goods have names and designations, but where the wish draws its deepest breath, where this unknown seems to manifest itself, there is wonder,[19] and wonder is immediacy's sense of God and is the beginning of all deeper understanding. The seeking of the wishing person is in the dark not so much in regard to the object, because this is indeed the unknown, as in regard to whether he is getting closer to it or further away—now he is startled and the expression of his wonder is worship. Wonder is an ambivalent state of mind containing both fear and blessedness. Worship therefore is simultaneously a mixture of fear and blessedness. Even the most purified, reasonable worship is blessedness in fear and trembling, trust in mortal danger, bold confidence in the consciousness of sin. Even the most purified and reasonable worship of God has the fragility of wonder, and the magnitude of the God-relation is not directly determined by the magnitude of power and of wisdom and of deed; the most powerful person is the most powerless; the most devout person sighs out of deepest distress; the most mighty is the one who rightly folds his hands.

The wonder of the wishing person corresponds to the unknown and thus is altogether indefinable or, rather, is infinitely
definable; it can be just as loathsome as it is ludicrous, just as
erring as it is childish. When the forest frowns at eventide,
when the night's moon gets lost in the trees, when the natural
wonder in it is on the prowl for its booty and then the pagan
suddenly sees the marvel of a luminous effect that grips him,
then he sees the unknown, and worship is the expression of
wonder. When the gnarled trunk creates an illusive figure that
is unfamiliar to him, that resembles a human being and yet
again, to his amazement, resembles it only larger than life, then
he stands still and worships. When he is out in the desert and
sees a track that does not belong to any human being or any
creature known to him, when the power of solitude impreg-
nates his soul with wonder, then he sees in this track that the
unknown has been here, and he worships. When the ocean lies
deep and still and inexplicable, when wonder stares dizzily          V
down into it until it seems as if the unknown is rising to the      186
surface, when the waves roll monotonously against the beach
and overwhelm the soul by the power of the monotony, when
the rushes whisper before the wind and whisper again and
therefore must want to confide something to the listener, then
he worships.

If the wonder defines itself, then its highest expression is that
God is the inexplicable all of existence as this is intimated to the
power of the imagination everywhere in the least and the greatest. The content of paganism is experienced again in the repetition of each generation, and not until it is lived through is that
which was idolatry reduced to a carefree being in the innocence
of poetry. Idolatry purified is the poetic.

If the person wishing is himself assumed to be able to contribute something to finding what is sought, then he is striving. Then the wonder and the wish are in the process of under-
going their test. Often deceived, since the range of wonder,
precisely because it was related directly to the unknown, was
just as loathsome as it was ludicrous, just as erring as it was
childish—often deluded, wonder wants to see where it is going
and no longer walk in the dark. In this way the direct relation is

at the outset a broken relation, yet the break is not a breakthrough. It is broken inasmuch as the road intervenes as a
determinant, whereas for the person wishing there is no road.
When the seeker is not walking in the dark, he is not merely
wishing, he is striving, because striving is the very road to
what is sought.[20] Everyone was once like that in early youth,
lofty of flight in willing—alas, even if many have now learned
to keep their feet on the ground, have they all therefore also
become wiser, also the person who instead of winning the
flight of the bird won the stooping gait of the four-footed!
Everyone was once like that in early youth, reckless in
venturing—alas, even if many abandoned that, did they all
therefore also become wiser, also the person who instead of
winning the race of recklessness on the course of the unknown
won the security of the pedestrian on the highway of mediocrity! Everyone was once like that in early youth, aggressively
challenging—alas, even if many learned to tone down their
demands, did they all therefore become wiser, also the person
who became surfeited through preferential treatment, or the
person who learned pettiness from his environment, or the
person who in the bondage of habits learned contentment with
little! Oh, surely it is wisest not to speak of good fortune if we
know something holier to name, but if not, then it would of
course be a misfortune if good fortune vanished from life, if it
became weary of giving and taking, weary of people who
defrauded it out of wonder.

V
187

But in the world of freedom, where all striving indeed has its
source and in which all striving has its life, there wonder appears on the road. Endeavor has various names, but that which
is directed toward the unknown is directed toward God. That it
is directed toward the unknown means that it is infinite. Then
the striving one comes to a standstill; he sees the illusive track
of an enormous being that exists when it is gone, that is and is
not. And this being is fate, and his striving is akin to going
astray. Worship is again the expression of wonder, and the
range of worship is just as loathsome as it is ludicrous, just as
erring as it is childish.

If the seeker is assumed to be able to do everything to find what is sought, the enchantment is gone, the wonder forgotten; there is nothing to wonder over. [21]And then in the next moment what is sought is a nothing, and that was why he was capable of everything. Everyone was once like that at youth's turn of the year—then he became an eternity old.[22] Alas, although many console themselves over not having experienced this horror, have they all therefore become wiser, also the one who was a youth in his old age! Everyone has experienced at some time, at the departure of youth, that life stood still and he perished; and although many nevertheless boast of their youth, was that one wiser who defrauded the years and eternity of their rights, whose highest wisdom was a flippant answer to the most earnest question!

There was a time in the world when humankind, weary of wonder, weary of fate, turned away from the external and discovered that there was no object of wonder, that the unknown was a nothing and wonder a deception. What once was life's substance comes again in the repetition of the race. If anyone thinks he is wise when he says that there are bygone formations finished and done with thousands of years ago, it is not this way in life. And you certainly do not think either, my listener, that I would waste your time by telling about great events, mentioning quaint names, and becoming inanely self-important in a consideration of the whole human race! Alas, no, if it is true that the person who comes to know a little is deceived, is he not also deceived who comes to know so much that he appropriated nothing whatever! Humankind progresses slowly; even the most glorious knowledge is still only a presupposition. If one wishes to increase the presuppositions, then one is indeed like the miser who amasses money for which he has no use. Even what is deserving of being highly valued, a happy upbringing, even that is only a presupposition and appropriating it takes time, and a whole lifetime is not too much if one wants to appropriate it. Ah, if the one whose upbringing was neglected was deceived, was he not also deceived who remained ignorant of the fact that it was a presupposition, a trust, a sacred heritage that should be acquired, and who abruptly took it and thought himself to be what he had the name for being.

If at times a better one sighed because what was sought was so far away, you, my listener, certainly have grasped that there is also another difficulty, that there is a phantom of knowledge that fascinates the soul, that there is a security in which one is knowing—and yet deceived, that there is a distance from all decision where one, without dreaming it, is lost. Let terror seize its prey—ah, this security is a more terrible monster! Let the distress of want starve out—is it better to perish from superabundance? It was shocking when wonder abandoned a person and he despaired over himself, but it is equally shocking that one can know about this, know much more, and not even have experienced this, and it is most shocking that someone can know everything and not have made a beginning on the least thing. If this is the case, ah, then let me begin all over again. Turn back, you youth, with your wishing and your endearing wonder; turn back, you wild striving of youth, with your recklessness and your trembling before that unknown. Seize me, you despair, which breaks with wonder and the wonder of youth, but quickly, quickly. If it is possible, if I have wasted my best time without experiencing anything, at least teach me in so doing not to become indifferent, teach me not to seek the consolation of others in a common loss; then surely the terror of the loss may be a beginning of my healing. However late it is, this is still better than to go on living as a liar, deceived not by what could seem calculated to deceive, alas, and for this reason dreadfully deceived—deceived by much knowledge!

[23]So the wonder was gone; it is gone. So it was once said; this is what the despairing one says and repeats in despair, repeats it mockingly, and wants to console himself by means of mockery, although this mockery wounds others, as if all mockery were not two-edged! But you, my listener, you of course know that the discourse has just now come to the true wonder. The discourse will therefore not take you by surprise; neither will it deceive you by means of an optical illusion when the lightning

of thought flashes as everything is reversed; neither will it sweep you away in startled confusion. The one who actually has experienced the above readily sees through the confused mingling of recollections, and if he has not experienced it, then hearing or reading a discourse will be of only doubtful value to him. But you who are yourself in a state of wonder, you of course know that this wonder came into existence when at some time that first wonder was consumed in despair.

But what more worthy object of wonder is to be found than the person who, seeking in wish and endeavor, perishing in despair, suddenly discovered that he has what is sought and the misfortune is that he is standing there and losing it! Take the wisher as he sits there and dreams; call to him and say, "You have what you wished for." Stop the reckless striver as he rushes down the road; stop him and say, "You have what was coveted." Break through the despair so that the despairing one perceives that he has what is sought. How agitated he will be when he is simultaneously overwhelmed by wonder and is overwhelmed because he in turn seems to lose what is sought! The glory of the wish and the reckless striving do not reawaken wonder; the dash [*Tankestreg*, thought-line] of despair prevents it. But that what is sought is given, that it is possessed by the person who in misunderstanding stands there and is losing it— that awakens the wonder of the whole person. Indeed, what more powerful expression of wonder is there than for the wonderer to become as if changed, than for the wisher to change color; what more powerful expression than this, that he *actually* becomes changed! And so it is with this wonder—it changes the seeker; and so it is with this change—it seeks to become something else, indeed, become the very opposite: to seek means that the seeker himself is changed. He is not to look for the place where the object of his seeking is, because it is right with him; he is not to look for the place where God is, he is not to strive to get there, because God is right there with him, very near, everywhere near, at every moment everywhere present, but the seeker must be changed so that he himself can become the place where God in truth is.

V
189

Wonder, however, which is the beginning of all deeper understanding, is an ambivalent passion that in itself contains fear and blessedness. Or was it not fearful, my listener, that what was sought was so close to you, that you did not seek but God sought you? Was it not fearful that you could not stir without being in him, could not be still without being in him, could not be so unnoticed that you were not in him, and could not flee to the farthest limits of the world[24] without his being there and everywhere along the way, could not hide in the abyss without his being there and everywhere along the way, and could not say to him, "In a moment," because he also was in the moment when you said this? Was it not fearful when the jesting of youth and the immaturity of despair became earnestness, when what you had pointed to and hankered for and said did not exist came into existence, indeed, when it existed everywhere around you and surrounded you on all sides! But was it not blessed that the powerful one could confine you in the darkest nook and yet could not shut God out? Was it not blessed that you could fall into the deepest abyss where one sees neither the sun nor the stars and yet can see God? Was it not blessed that you could go astray in the lonely desert and yet immediately find the way to God? Was it not blessed that you could become an old man who had forgotten everything and yet never forget God because he cannot become something past, that you could become mute and still call to him, deaf and still hear him, blind and still see him? Was it not blessed that you dare to rely upon him, that he would not say as we human beings say, "In a moment," because he was with you the moment he said it!

But the person who leaves out the fear, let him see to it that he does not leave out the discovery. It is so easy—or if someone prefers saying the same thing in another way—it is so hard to find God that one even demonstrates that he exists and finds a demonstration necessary.[25] Let the work of demonstrating be hard, let it in particular give trouble to the person who is to understand that it demonstrates something. For the one who is demonstrating it is an easy matter, because he has come to stand on the outside and is not dealing with God but is discussing something about God. If, however, seeking is to mean that one is oneself changed, then let the seeker look to himself. One learns wonder from a child and fear from an adult; this is always a preparation. Then the fear does indeed come along with God when he comes and makes demonstrations superfluous. Or is it perhaps courage to go on being thoughtlessly unaware of the danger, that the one who is demonstrating remains unchanged and demonstrates over and over that the Omnipresent One exists, the Omnipresent One who even in the moment of demonstration [26]sees through the one doing the demonstrating—without, however, having any scholarly judgment on the merit of the demonstration. Can the Omnipresent One actually have become like a rare natural phenomenon whose existence the scientist demonstrates, or like a variable star observed at century-long intervals and whose existence therefore requires demonstration, especially during the intervening centuries when it is not seen!

But one human being cannot teach another true wonder and true fear. Only when they compress and expand your soul—yours, yes yours, yours alone in the whole world, because you have become alone with the Omnipresent One—only then are they in truth for you.[27] If a speaker had the eloquence of an angel and if he had a countenance that could strike terror into the bravest of brave, so that you fell, as is said, into the most profound wonder at his eloquence and horror gripped you in hearing him, it is not that wonder and it is not that fear that helps. In relation to every human being, the lowliest and the greatest, it holds true that not an angel and not legions of angels and not the horrors of the whole world can impart true wonder and true fear, but they certainly can make him superstitious. There are true wonder and true fear only when he, he himself, the lowliest or the greatest, comes to be alone with the Omnipresent One. The magnitude of the power and wisdom and deed do not define the actual magnitude of the relationship. Did not the seers in Egypt perform almost as great signs as Moses?[28] Suppose that they had performed greater signs; what would follow from that? Nothing, absolutely nothing with regard to the God–relationship. But Moses feared God, and Moses was filled with wonder over God, and the fear and the wonder or the wonder's fear and its blessedness determine the magnitude of the God-relationship.

What the understanding says is quite true—namely, that there is nothing to wonder about, but for this very reason wonder is safeguarded—because the understanding vouches for it. Just let the understanding judge what is perishable, let it clear out the place—then wonder comes to the right place in the changed individual. The understanding is able to dispose of everything that belonged to that first wonder; let it do so in order that it can enigmatically help one to the wonder, because it is indeed enigmatic, since it directly conflicts with the understanding's judgment of itself. But if a person advances no further, then let him not accuse the understanding nor celebrate because it has been victorious. If a prince sends a captain with a battalion of soldiers against a foreign country and that captain conquers it and then takes possession of it himself as a rebel, there is no reason to accuse him because he conquered it, but neither is there reason to celebrate because he kept it for himself—similarly, if by way of his understanding a person conquers what certainly was beautiful but yet also childish, let him not accuse understanding, but if the understanding ends with inciting mutiny, then let him not celebrate. But the wonder is in the one who is changed.

What has been said here has certainly happened to everyone at some time in the moment of decision, when sickness of spirit struck inward and he felt trapped in existence, trapped forever. Alas, even if many console themselves on having avoided this danger, was that person therefore also wiser who cunningly and cravenly deceived himself when he thought he was deceiving God and life! Something like this has happened at some time to everyone when it was over with jesting and delusion and diversion. Alas, even if many boast of their freedom from care, did that person therefore also become wiser whose life grew wild as a sucker side-shoot because he was not bound! [29]Something like this has happened at some time to everyone, alas, and even if many indulge in more advantageous conditions, did that person therefore become wiser who, unbound, did not know that for that very reason he was unfree!

If what is sought is assumed to be given, seeking means that the seeker himself is changed and becomes the place where what is sought can be present in truth. What was sought was indeed given; it was so close that it was as if lost again. Indeed, what stronger expression for consternation is there than this, that it seems to be lost without the certainty that it is lost—this, then, is how a person goes backward! What a distance since that time when he wished, when he recklessly ventured, when what was sought was far away, when the egotism challenged its nonexistence—and now it has come so close to him that it is lost, and with the loss it recedes far away into the distance!

The seeker was to be changed, and he was changed, alas—in this way it goes backward. And the change in which he is we call sin. Therefore, what was sought is; and the seeker is the place, but is changed, changed from once having been the place where the object of his seeking was. Ah, now there is no wonder, no ambivalence! The condition of the soul when it comprehends this is fear and trembling in the guilty one; the passion is sorrow after recollection; the love is repentance in the prodigal.

My listener, was it not like that! After all, the discourse will surely not take you by surprise; it has no authority to extort any confession of sin from you. On the contrary, it willingly admits its powerlessness in this regard. Indeed, if anyone desires that, it is quite willing to tell him that all the eloquence of the world is unable to convince a person of his guilt, but then will also remind him not to fear the eloquence of sinners but the omnipresence of the Holy One, and even more to fear to avoid the Holy One. If a person is to understand his sin essentially, he must understand it because he becomes alone, he alone, just he alone, with the Holy One, who knows everything. Only this fear and trembling is the true fear and trembling, only the grief that the recollection of God awakens in a person, only the repentance his love loves forth. If a speaker had a voice like the thunder of the heavens, a countenance that struck terror, if he knew how to aim with his eyes, and now as you sat there, my listener, he pointed at you and said, "You, there, you are a sinner," and even did it with such force that your eyes dropped to the ground and the blood drained from your cheeks and you perhaps did not recover from the impact for a long time, then you certainly would realize that in so behaving he was transforming the setting into a burlesque theater, where he played the buffoon, and you would deplore his having disturbed you in finding stillness. Fear and trembling before something repulsive, before someone religiously profligate, is not true fear and trembling. Just as a person should not seek his peace through another human being and should not build upon sand, so it also holds true that he should not rely on any other person's work to convince him that he is a sinner, but rather to remind him of his own responsibility before God if he does not discover it by himself—any other understanding is diversion. It is only a jest if I would pass judgment on you, but it is a serious matter if you forget that God will pass the judgment.

So what is sought is given. God is near enough, but no one *without purity* can *see God*, and sin is impurity, *and therefore no one can become aware of God without becoming a sinner.* The first is a beckoning word, and the gaze of the soul is toward the heights where the goal is, but other words that provide the beginning are immediately heard, and these are depressing words. And yet this is the way it is for the person who wants to understand sin. An unauthorized discourse cannot hope to convince anyone—indeed, it cannot even directly benefit anyone. The person who feels himself to be the stronger cannot possibly be vanquished by the discourse, and the person who lets himself be overcome shows in that very way that he was the stronger. Therefore the discourse refuses to impose upon you, my listener, or put anything over on you. On the contrary, it gives you instead a weapon to use against the speaker if you would be so foolish as to want to pass judgment on him, which would certainly be thoughtless, whereas it is a serious matter if someone forgets to accuse himself before God. For this reason, you will not learn very much from the discourse; if you come to know something about yourself from it, that is your own doing; but if someone demanded to obtain some knowledge about sin in general, he would be demanding too much from the discourse, because then he would be deceived.

So the discourse now stands at the beginning. This does not happen through wonder, but truly not through doubt either, because the person who doubts his guilt is only making a bad beginning, or rather he is continuing what was badly begun with sin. What comes with sin is accompanied by sorrow; and this certainly is true of sin itself. Therefore sorrow is the beginning, and the trembling is sorrow's vigilance. The more profound the sorrow is, the more a person feels himself as a nothing, as less than nothing, and this happens simply because the sorrower is the seeker who is beginning to become aware of God. It has always been said, even in paganism, that the gods do not sell the highest for nothing, that a divine envy wherein divinity set a price upon itself determined the conditions of the relationship.[30] Why, then, should not this, as an individual human being to discover God, why should not this have its requirement, and this requirement is that the person become a sinner. And yet, if I dare to say so, it is not a polite courtesy the person shows him, that his holy presence reduces the single individual to a sinner; no, the single individual was that, but became that first through his presence.

V
194

But the person seeking to understand himself in the consciousness of sin before God does not understand it as a general statement that all people are sinners, because the emphasis is not on this generality. The more profound the sorrow is, the more a person feels himself as a nothing, as less than nothing, and this diminishing self-esteem is a sign that the sorrower is the seeker who is beginning to become aware of God. In a worldly sense, it holds true that it is a poor soldier who does not hope to become commander. In a religious sense, it is the opposite; the less a person thinks of himself, not as humanity in general or as a human being, but of himself as an individual human being, and not with regard to his talents but with regard to his guilt, the more manifest God becomes to him. We do not want to increase the guilt in order that God might become greater[31] but want to increase the acknowledgment of guilt. [32]Just as that authority who vigilantly watches over justice sometimes uses spies who are themselves guilty, likewise everyone the Holy One uses is himself a transgressor, at times a transgressor even in the strictest sense. Accordingly, the Holy One is concerned both about the salvation of the transgressor and about saving others through him.

The more profound the sorrow is, the more profoundly the power of sin is comprehended, and the strongest expression for the most profound sorrow might seem to be to feel oneself the greatest of sinners. As a matter of fact, in times when this has been the highest expression for the highest distinction, there has in a vain way even been argument and dispute about this rank, and people have done everything to win this recognition. Any kind of mistaken effort is lamentable, of course, but the most lamentable is religious debauchery. When a youth makes a mistake in life, one hopes for the years ahead; it is even more lamentable when an adult goes astray; but when someone goes astray in the ultimate that can save, where then is salvation! But it does not follow that it would be praiseworthy to postpone godly piety and thereby avoid the error. [33]The greatest sinner—and dispute about being that! We shall not burst into laughter despite the presence of a contradiction that justifies laughter, because even though it is laughable this is not the place to laugh at such a mixing of folly into a most serious connection.

Neither will the discourse promptly drop the expression but will dwell a little on it and ask, "How does a person get to know that he is the greatest of sinners?" If he gets to know that he is a sinner, he does so in this way, that he comes to be alone—he, he himself, alone with the Holy One. If he does not come to be alone in this way, he does not even find out that he is a sinner, to say nothing of being the greatest. What is the basis of the more or less by which he defines himself as the greatest? Does not this more come from evil; does it not come by way of fraud and deceit; is it not due to diversion from earnestness and to concentration on vanity? An unfortunate who became earnest through his suffering is promptly recognized by his judging, without being concerned whether others are suffering less: My suffering is oppressive for me—I am suffering. A true lover is recognized at once by his not defiling the lovers' tryst, which seeks solitude, by bringing along a crowd, a flock of witnesses, who are of course present as soon as he understands that he loves more than others. No, his honest and sincere judgment is brief: I am in love. And so it is also with the consciousness of sin—the simple statement is the most earnest. All comparison is worldly, all emphasis upon it is a worldly attachment in the service of vanity. Even worse than one's own guilt is one's own righteousness, and even worse than one's own righteousness is to take in vain the ultimate and in earnest to become the greatest of sinners by conceitedly wanting to be that. But the person who comes to be alone with the consciousness of sin will certainly feel, though not comparatively, that he is the greatest of sinners, because directly before the Holy One he will be conscious of himself as the single individual and of the essential magnitude of the sin within himself. If it is diversion to want to excuse oneself because others are more guilty, then it is also diversion to want to determine one's sin by its relation to the sin of others, which, however, no one knows. But when you fast, my listener, anoint your head and wash your face;[34] then for diversion you will not see either that others are more guilty or that others are less guilty; and you do not do on the street something that is not a joint enterprise but do it properly in secret.

Ah, it is much easier to look to the right and to the left than to look into oneself, much easier to haggle and bargain just as it is also much easier to underbid than to be silent—but the more difficult is still the one thing needful. Even in daily life everyone experiences that it is more difficult to stand directly before the person of distinction, directly before his royal majesty, than to move in the crowd; to stand alone and silent directly before the sharp expert is more difficult than to speak in a common harmony of equals—to say nothing of being alone directly before the Holy One and being silent.

V
196

People see God in great things, in the raging of the elements and in the course of world history; they entirely forget what the child understood, that when it shuts its eyes it sees God. When the child shuts its eyes and smiles, it becomes an angel; alas, when the adult comes to be alone before the Holy One and is silent—he becomes a sinner! First of all, be alone; then you will

indeed learn the proper worship of God, to think highly of God
and lowly of yourself—not more lowly than your neighbor, as
if you were the distinguished one (but remember that you are
before God)—not more lowly than your enemy, as if you were
the better one (for remember that you are before God); but
lowly of yourself.

Anyone who thinks of his sin in this way and wishes in this
stillness to learn an art—something you, my listener, do not
disdain, the art of sorrowing over his sins—will certainly discover that the confession of sin is not merely a counting of all
the particular sins but is a comprehending before God that sin
has a coherence in itself. But here again he will pay attention to
the narrow way,[35] because the way of the solitary one is narrow
and inclosed, but everywhere there are blind doors. He needs
only to say a word and one of them opens—and the prisoner
breathes in the open; so it seems to him for a moment. For
example, if he begins to talk about the universality of sin, not in
him but in the whole human race, if he snatches at this thought,
a door opens—alas, and how easily he now breathes, he whose
breathing was so labored; how easy now his escape, he whose
gait was so arduous; how free he now becomes, he who was
hard-working—because he has become an observer.[36] And
many are very eager to hear his observations.[37] In this way the
matter becomes something different, so easy, so changed—
indeed, changed in the way the earnest one among us says it,[38]
that the issue becomes the justifying of God before the world,
not a concern about justifying oneself before God. To confess
one's sin in general is easier, but from the particular sin, which
is precisely and definitely apprehended, meticulously as an im-
partial judge draws it up, from this particular or these particular sins to discover a coherence is a hard course and a mandatory course, but the hard course is still the right course, and the
mandatory course is the beneficial one.

There is a quality that is highly praised but not easily acquired: it is honesty. I am not talking about that charming
honesty of children, which is certainly to be found also in some
adults, because to praise that, my listener, would deceive you
with the discourse. If it is found in you, the discourse would

then become almost flattering, even if your childlikeness would prevent you from understanding it as such. And if it is not found, then it would mock you. The discourse will therefore not make distinctions and pander to you and pretend that honesty is a fortunate gift to the infant in the cradle that only few receive. Such a discourse belongs where fortune separates people, not where the God-relationship recognizes equality. No, honesty is a duty, and everyone is supposed to have it. But it is difficult to acquire it amid much diversion. I do not mean that a person is therefore promptly a liar, but he does not gain the time and the collectedness to understand himself. Is not this the way it is? A person wishes something, fervently wishes it, or so he thinks; meanwhile much happens before the wish is fulfilled, or fulfillment does not come at all, and he has changed. It is certainly possible that he has become wiser, but his wisdom still lacks one thing, a definite impression that he once wished it, and not a fanciful piece of information about his having wished it a few years ago but now he does not. For the two states of mind to be reconciled beautifully and harmoniously in the unity of the same soul, it is necessary that they have a little meeting in which they make themselves understandable to each other.

Wisdom is perhaps all right, but perhaps the wise person lacks a little sorrow over himself. A person now resolves something definite, but time haggles and he is changed, and it becomes a half-measure. Perhaps the resolution was actually too ambitious for his capacities. Well, but a little something is still lacking here, a little distress, a little clarity as to whether it was time that had given the person the appearance of wisdom or whether he actually had become wiser. And now guilt and error and sin! Ah, how many there are who years later know definitely what they wished, what they resolved, what they reproached themselves for, what offense they had committed! And God can certainly require honesty of a person. How much more difficult this becomes! A person can actually strive in all honesty to become more and more transparent to himself, but would he dare to present this clarity to a knower of hearts as something positively trustworthy between himself and him?

V
197

Far from it! Even the person who inwardly strives honestly, even that person, and perhaps he most of all, will always have an outstanding account that he is not confident of being able to settle, whether he did not actually have a greater, at times in particular instances perhaps a smaller, debt than he thinks. And this is probably the best. A person still has only one God, and if he does not get along with him, to whom shall he go? Note here the necessity of understanding from the particular sin and error that there is a coherence, an unfathomable coherence.

If someone were to say to you, my listener, that it may be utterly useless to want to achieve honesty, because even the person who is trying most honestly always remains somewhat hazy to himself, then do as the speaker does—be as one who has not heard it at all. The speaker is certainly no sprinter, but neither is he about to let himself procrastinate because of cowardice or because of cowardly envy that wants to have equality in mediocrity and to have spiritual fervor transformed into somnolence and to have enthusiasm that serves without pay transformed into an association of plain profit. You are well aware, my listener, that there is this miserableness that cannot tolerate anything better, that there is this perfidious friendship that wants to procrastinate; but do not struggle with them. That is still not the place where you are to struggle—to struggle with them is already a victory for them. Seek instead the forgetfulness of silence; in it you will come to know something entirely different about your own guilt!

Thus honesty is difficult. It is easier to hide in the crowd and to drown one's guilt in that of the human race, easier to hide from oneself than to become open in honesty before God. As said earlier, this honesty is certainly not a perpetual enumerating, but neither is it the signing [*Underskrift*] of a name on a piece of white paper, a signed confession to an empty generality; and a confessor [*Skriftende*] is not a co-signatory in the human race's enormous account book.

But without honesty there is no repentance. Repentance is nauseated by the empty generality, but it is not a petty arithmetician in the service of faintheartedness—rather an earnest observer before God. To repent of a generality without substance is a contradiction, akin to inviting the most profound passion to dine on superficiality, but to tie one's repentance to a particular is to repent on one's own responsibility and not before God, and to vitiate the intention is self-love in depression. Is it so easy to repent: to love and to feel one's wretchedness ever more deeply, to love while the punishment is being suffered, to love and not want to falsify the punishment as divine dispensation, to love and not want to hide secret resentment as if one suffered an injustice, to love and not want to stop seeking the sacred source of this pain!

Anyone who thinks about his sin also knows that there is a difference between sins. This, of course, he knows from what he learned from his catechism, and everyone thinks best about this by himself. It has surely happened in this world that through a discourse that described sin in general in dreadful colors one recognized a dreadful connection with a particular sin. But religious debauchery is still the most dreadful of all. A discourse of that kind may have scared the more pure and created an anxiety, a continuing anxiety, in the soul of the more innocent. But what is the point of the speaker's terrifying—only the person himself understands that he is guilty. The person who does not understand it this way still misunderstands; and the person who does understand it will find the harsh or gentle or quickly sympathizing explanation, according to what he has deserved.

V
199

But it is still detestable if anyone, because he must personally bear the heavy punishment for the more terrible sin, would want to derive advantage from this for a new sin: to be able to terrify. Alas, the indulgence of light-mindedness is certainly a new sin, but the ungodly imposition of dark passions is surely also a new sin![39] And you, my listener, you of course know that earnestness is to be alone before the Holy One, whether it is the world's applause that is shut out or whether it is the world's accusation that withdraws. Did the woman who was a sinner[40] feel her guilt more deeply when the scribes were accusing her than when there was no accuser anymore and she stood alone before the Lord! But you also realize that the most dangerously deceived person is the one who is self-deceived, that the most dangerous condition is that of the one who is deceived by much knowledge, and, furthermore, that it is a lamentable weakness to have one's consolation in another's light-mindedness, but it is also a lamentable weakness to have one's terror from another's heavy-mindedness. Leave it solely to God—after all, he knows best how to take care of everything for one who becomes alone by seeking him.

—And there is indeed a place for this, my listener, and you know where; and there is indeed an opportunity, my listener, and you know how; and there is indeed a moment, and it is called: this very day.

Here this discourse ends—in the confession of sin. But can it really be an end? Is joy not to be victorious now; is sin to walk only with sorrow; is the soul to sit oppressed but is the harp of joy not to be tuned?[41] You perhaps are accustomed to hearing much more; you probably know much more yourself—so look for the shortcoming in the discourse and the speaker. If you actually are further along, then do not let yourself be delayed, but if not, then consider that one is dreadfully deceived if one is deceived by much knowledge. Let us imagine a first mate and assume that he has passed with distinction all the examinations but as yet has not been out to sea. Imagine him in a storm: he knows exactly what he has to do, but he is unacquainted with the terror that grips the sailor when the stars disappear into the pitch darkness of the night; he is unacquainted with the sense of powerlessness the pilot feels when he sees that the helm in his hand is only a plaything for the sea; he does not know how the blood rushes to the head when in such a moment one must make calculations—in short, he has no conception of the change that takes place in the knower when he is to use his knowledge. What fair weather is for the sailor, going on living at the same pace with others and with the generation is for the individual person, but the decision, the dangerous moment of collecting himself when he is to withdraw from the surroundings and become alone before God and become a sinner—this is a stillness that changes the ordinary just as the storm does. He knows it all, knows what is to happen to him, but he did not know the anxiety that grips him when he feels himself abandoned by the multiplicity in which he had his soul; he did not know how the heart pounds when the help of others and the guidance of others and the standards of others and the diversions of others vanish in stillness; he did not know the shuddering when it is too late to call for human help, when no one can hear him—in short, he had no conception of how the knower is changed when he is to appropriate his knowledge.

Is it perhaps also the case with you, my listener? I certainly do not judge you; I merely ask. Alas, although there come to be more and more who know so very much, experienced people are becoming more and more rare! But it was exactly that kind of person you once wished to be. You surely have not forgotten what we said about honesty toward oneself—that one distinctly remembers what one once wished to be; and you yourself surely intended to be honest before God in the confession of sins. What was it you wanted then? You wanted to strive for the highest, to grasp the truth and be in it; you wanted to spare neither time nor effort; you wanted to renounce everything, including also every deception. Even if you did not grasp the highest, you still wanted to be sure that you were clearly aware of what you hitherto had understood its attainment to be. Even if this were ever so little, you still would rather be faithful over little than faithless over much.[42] Even if it were one single thought and you became the poor one among the rich who know everything, you still would rather be true as gold[43]—and indeed everyone can be that if he so wishes, inasmuch as gold does indeed belong to the rich, but the poor can also be true as gold. The person who was faithful over little, faithful on that day of distress when the accounting is made, faithful in understanding his debt, faithful in the stillness in which no reward beckons but the guilt becomes clear, faithful in the honesty that acknowledges everything, even that this honesty is deficient, faithful in penitent love, the humble love whose claim is self-accusation—he will certainly be placed over more.[44]

Was not this the way you wanted it? We do agree, do we not, that in regard to what is essential *to be able* essentially means *to be able to do* it. The child thinks differently, and when the little

V
201

fellow is learning what has been assigned to him and then perhaps asks his big sister to hear him recite it but she is busy and answers, "No, my dear boy, I do not have time now, but read the lesson five times or read it ten times and sleep on it, and tomorrow you will know it perfectly," the child believes it, does as he is told, and the next day knows it perfectly. But the more mature person learns in another way. If someone were to memorize the Bible, there could be something beautiful inasmuch as there was something childlike in his behavior, but essentially the adult learns only by appropriating, and he essentially appropriates the essential only by doing it.

Oh, in the midst of all the distress, what beautiful joy in life, in the human race, in being human oneself! Oh, in the stillness, what beautiful harmony with everyone! Oh, in this solitude, what beautiful fellowship with everyone! It is not true that one human being does not have the same essential task as another human being, any more than one human being's outward appearance is essentially different from another's, but each one does understand it a bit differently and in his own way. There are not, as in confusion, different roads and different truths and new truths, but there are many roads leading to the one truth and each person walks his own. The distinctiveness [*Eiendom-melighed*] arises when the essential becomes the possession [*Eiendom*] of the single individual and this distinctiveness is conditioned by doing the essential and is discovered in that way. Is it the aim of this discourse to be divisive? Far be it from this discourse to mention the distinctiveness for which there is struggling in the world, just as for other gifts of fortune. No, everyone who possesses something essential by having done it has possession and distinctiveness.

So also, to recall the subject of the discourse, to understand that stillness means to be able to become still. Where does one become still? Well, there is a place for that, but not in the external and direct sense, because the place is of no avail if one does not bring stillness along. In a certain sense, then, there is no place—ah, is not this "in a certain sense" already disquieting! When does one most need this stillness? When one is most powerfully moved. Is not this thought capable of driving the stillness away? Where, then, does one flee [*flye*] in order to escape [*undflye*] from oneself? Indeed, if one wishes to flee, one escapes this very stillness! Is there nothing at all to do, then? Well, if one wishes to do nothing at all, one again escapes from the stillness into the stillness of spiritual death. Is it so easy to be able to become still! Now security tempts, because there is of course plenty of time; now impatience, because it is too late; now a beckoning hope, now a lingering recollection; now a wild resolution, now an echo of public opinion that mockingly overtakes you as if you were going down this road of stillness into the desert of illusion, where the solitary one perishes; now an echo from the selfishness in you that disturbs with self-admiration; now a comparison that diverts; now an estimate that diverts, now a little forgetfulness with the help of thoughtlessness; now a little advance payment with the help of self-confidence, now a fanciful notion of God's infinitude; now dejection over having to confide to the All-knowing One what he knows anyway, now a light-minded leap that avails nothing; now a heavy-minded sigh that feeds the heavy-mindedness, now a little sadness that anesthetizes; now a clarity that amazes, now a stillness by means of plans and ideas and daydreams and flights of fancy instead of a stillness by means of guilt and an accounting and intention's covenant with the obvious guilt and the omniscient God.

Is it so easy to become still! To have been so very close to it and yet to have grasped an illusion and to have to begin again and therefore with more unrest! To have found consolation with another and then to discover that it was a self-deception, a fraudulent stillness, and therefore to have to begin with more unrest! To have been disturbed by the world, by an enemy, by a friend, by a false teacher, by a hypocrite, by a mocker, and then to discover that it is a self-deception to want to shove the guilt upon someone else, and therefore to have to begin with more unrest! To have struggled, to will with all one's power, and then to discover that one is capable of nothing, that one cannot give oneself this stillness because it belongs to God! If someone declares that this is the correct expression, that one cannot do it, then perhaps let him consider carefully whether it is laziness

V
202

that is speaking here. Indeed it is true; yes, even an apostle witnesses to it, but was this testimony a whim, a hasty general comment, or was it not so difficult to understand this human nothingness and to have one's consciousness in it that even he, the authoritative one, the eternally resolved one, was not alone in it but needed a helper, namely, a Satan's angel, who by means of daily experiences and daily pain helped him out of illusion,[45] out of having his wisdom in rote learning, his peace in general assurances, his trust in God in a saying. Or had someone taught the apostle this, so he could repeat it? We certainly have heard before in the world that the wise man had an angel who guided or warned him.[46] If Paul had spoken of this, it could have been by rote, but that the wise man needs a Satan's angel for his daily use, that certainly has taken a long time to learn.

Yet the discourse must not be divisive. What God requires of each one is best left to God. When the poor person or the person who works like a slave for a miserable living for himself and his family, and when the servant, most of whose time belongs to someone else, when these—alas, as it perhaps seems to them—have little opportunity to be able to consider the concerns of the soul, who could doubt, who would be brash and presumptuous enough, instead of having sympathy for this dissimilarity in earthly life, even to want to introduce it into the religious; who would dare to deny—that the blessing, like all God's blessings, is in abundance! But, my listener, if anyone, attacked by that fashionable sickness, had a loathing for existence and in intellectual pride disdained the simple and feared lest there not be tasks enough for his many thoughts, do you not think then that the wondrousness of truth is that the simple person understands it and the wisest person cannot wholly fathom it, and he does not become lazy on account of this thought but enthusiastic. Indeed, in this we are again agreed, inasmuch as this, too, is understood in stillness, where everyone has enough to think about by becoming guilty.

# On the Occasion of a Wedding

INEXPLICABLE moods seem to rest in the depths of the soul alongside the beautiful assurance of erotic love [*Elskov*[1]]; the organ music has now stopped; only the echo again stirs the soul in mood and wants to transfigure the beautiful assurance into a sacred mood—now is the time for speaking! The voice of an individual must be heard. How poor the word from the individual's lips might seem here in comparison with the beautiful and sacred emotion of rich moods. Might not the word at this point be disturbing, the well-intentioned word inopportune, the instructive even ominous! Yet it must be said—and it must be spoken with definiteness. The indefinable wealth of mood must be indicated; the word must be named; clarity, even if it has no desire to disturb anything, demands the word to the very end. What a change, what a relation in this misrelation! What is so plain and precise and distinct as a person's duty is and ought to be, and what is so puzzling as the prompting of love [*Kjærlighed*]—and yet here love is to become a duty! What is more transparent and intended for the future than a sacred promise, and what is less preoccupied with the future than the presence of erotic love in the lovers—and yet here a promise is required of love. What is so terrible to name as a curse,[2] and what is so remote from this as the sheer joy of erotic love—and yet the word must be named in connection with love!

But it is a free matter, and just as the lovers were set free by belonging to each other, so also is this step a resolution in freedom. There must, therefore, be joy with the joyful ones whom love made free in union, but there must be no speaking about the wedding with half words or scant words, as if it were something insignificant, because it belongs to freedom; accordingly, it is on the contrary the one thing needful in connection with the most beautiful happiness.

So now these two whom life united in the happiness of love have made a resolution, and now a covenant is to be made. A covenant for eternity. For eternity—is not this phrase so strong that it is almost ominous, because it is as if death intervened, and out there on the grave one lays eternity's wreath. Far from

it, inasmuch as the prophetic word is the beautiful word of
announcement. Indeed, the wedding ceremony is like a wreath
of eternity, but love weaves it, and duty says it must be woven;
and love's delight is to weave it, and duty says it must be
woven—every day from the flower of the moment. Here eternity is not finished with time, but the covenant is eternity's
beginning in time; the eternal resolution and the duty for eternity must remain with the wedded pair in the union of love
through time, and there is to be celebration at its remembrance
and power in its recollection and hope in its promise.

With definiteness, then, the word is to be spoken, and so it is
to be spoken with authority. And the discourse will address
itself to you, honorable bridegroom; it will not be congratula-
tory but will question with earnestness, and the speaker has the
authority to require an earnest answer. The discourse will not
ask about your happiness but will ask whether you have consulted God and your conscience. It will not scare your joy
away—no more than it is indifferent toward it. No, it wants
only to safeguard the joy for you if you answer with deliberation, and for your own sake it will earnestly ask that you do not
answer light-mindedly. And even if it seems to you to be so
natural, so altogether right that you be united to the one with
whom your parents and family initially wished you to be
united, to whom you belonged in a presentiment that quietly
became certainty, to whom you were drawn in so many ways
until love explicitly showed itself to be the foundation and took
your readiness into its transfiguring possession, the earnest
question here, far from desiring to stop an impetuous decision
of surprise, which too often results later in regret, will stop you
in order to place, with the responsibility of duty, the emphasis
of choice upon the quiet event.

Then the discourse will address itself to you, honored bride.
It will not make you uneasy with its questions or disquiet you
by awakening difficult thoughts, but it will ask with the same
earnestness—as required by the equality of the covenant—
whether you have consulted God and your conscience. Ah, the
question does not desire to make happiness precarious for you,
make you weak. It wants to make you in the freedom of ear-

nestness just as strong as the husband to whom you as wife are to be compliant. And even if you feel with joyous confidence and absolute reliability that happiness for you could not be otherwise or that it could not be in any other way than that you were united with him to whom you are linked by your life situation and close affinity and the sharing of so much in mutual understanding, until love explained the preceding as a beautiful introduction, as a dowry of security, as a wealth of happiness—the earnest question here, far from interrupting your many thoughts, will place for you, with the responsibility of duty, the emphasis of choice upon the quiet event's almost unnoticeable transition.

Thus a promise must be required, and the speaker has authority to demand it. Yet, for all its earnestness, the requirement is an invitation to the lovers; it wants to give the worthy ones the solemn occasion to express freely and before God what is difficult for the lovers to keep silent about with each other, what is delicious to confide to the confidant, what here pronounced is sanctified.

When this has happened, the authorized person will unite the married couple and make earnestness out of what is an earnest matter. It has its own earnestness, and when the bridal pair lack earnestness the act is debased, because the marriage ceremony is no temporal event. But when this earnestness is present, the authorized person makes earnestness of it—and the covenant is made.

An unauthorized discourse, however, has no lovers to unite. But despite that, my listener, you can readily heed it. As stated earlier, the act has its own earnestness, and the earnestness is not that something external takes place, that a few inquisitive people are eyewitnesses, that the life situation of two human beings is externally changed. And that earnestness indeed presupposes the authority in the married couple and that it is mature. If it first came into existence at that moment, who then would dare to answer the question that asks about something past, although it is also present? Or if the speaker was supposed to create the earnestness in the two lovers at that moment, he certainly would have to speak in a different way. He surely would have to say much that is risky to say now at the last moment, difficult to say to these two particular people, although it would have been beneficial if the two had thought about it. So there is a deliberation that in the earnestness of thought is now before the altar. To such a deliberation, then, I invite you, my listener, and with the wedding ceremony in mind I shall speak on the theme that, considered as the resolution of marriage,

## love conquers everything.

V
207

You, my listener, will of course also give thought to that earnest moment and not occupy your mind with the deliberation in any way except as it pertains to you, no matter whether your marriage covenant is something future or something past, inasmuch as it is of no concern only to a fool.[3] On this we surely do agree, that a discourse about godly things should never be divisive or at odds with anything except what is ungodly. Therefore when someone who is poor or earns his living in a menial job, without, of course, being excluded from the happiness of love, when he must glean laboriously and make many a burdensome attempt to gather the necessities, while the master or foreman perhaps understands all too well that the job has to be tended to first and foremost, when as a consequence there is only a snatched moment, a scrimpy time, for devoutly considering the affairs of the heart upon which the privileged and the pampered sometimes wisely, sometimes foolishly, spend so much time—therefore when these two lovers finally stand before the altar and in all brevity are pronounced legally married, ah, my listener, we certainly do agree that the God who is present in the covenant not merely to witness but also to bless, that his blessing does not make the distinction that human discourse makes. Because he is the only rich one, he has only one blessing, and the price is the same for everyone,[4] whether the believer is powerful or insignificant, wise or simple, dressed in gold or in coarse linsey-woolsey, rich in ideas or poor in spirit. But if anyone, man or woman, in the grip of that fashionable sickness, were so inhuman as to find this sacred practice along with its sacred rules too simple, if anyone has in mind the invention of something new, then we of course agree, my listener, that the wonder of this godly design is that the simple person finds everything in it and the wise person more than he can fathom if he earnestly thinks of himself in this relationship and thinks earnestly about himself.

An ancient saying states that love [*Kjærlighed*] is older than everything else,[5] and many a beautiful and many a profound thought is linked to this saying in order with its assistance to explain existence. But just as this saying is true in major matters, so is it also true wherever love is present: it is older than everything else. For example, in the life of the individual, when love awakens, it is older than everything else, because when it exists it seems as if it has existed for a long time; it presupposes itself back into the distant past until all searching ends in the inexplicable origin. Whereas all beginnings are ordinarily said to be difficult, this does not hold true of love's beginning. Its happy awakening is unacquainted with work, and there is no advance preparation. Even if love can give birth to pain, it is not brought forth in pain; lightly, jubilantly, it bursts forth in its enigmatic coming into existence. What a wonderful beginning!

V
208

But the life of freedom requires a beginning, and here a beginning is a resolution, and the resolution has its work and its pain—thus the beginning has its difficulty. The one making the resolution has, of course, not finished, because in that case he would have experienced that of which the resolution is the beginning. But if no resolution is made, the same thing can happen to such a person as sometimes happens to a speaker who only when he has finished speaking knows how he should have spoken: only when he has lived, only then does he know how he should have lived (what a sorry yield from life!) and how he should have made the beginning with the good resolution—what bitter wisdom now that a whole life lies between the beginning and the one who is dying!

Therefore the saying declares that love conquers everything, and this is why the wedding ceremony, which is no festive offering of congratulations but a godly invitation, does not greet the lovers as conquerors but invites them to conflict, fences them in the God-pleasing battleground of the state of marriage, encourages them to fight the good fight,[6] strengthens the contenders by means of the covenant, promises them victory as it accepts their promise, gives them the blessing for the long journey—but then also informs them that the conflict exists: a conflict that must be fought to the finish, toil that must be endured, danger that must be encountered, a curse if it is not jointly borne as a blessing.

But is this really the right place to evoke such sad observations, which will surely come soon enough along with the dark thoughts and the distressing experiences—in this moment of joy to call to mind the days that have no pleasure?[7] But is it sad, then, that this noble saying actually means something, that it is not sounding brass,[8] not the words of exultation over an imagined victory that is badly won, or at least badly won if it is already supposed to be won, but is the assurance of an actual victory that is to be won gloriously! Is the place so wrong, then? This holy place. Is it so inopportune for joy to think about the danger; is this perhaps not the time for it—in the rush of danger there surely will be less time! Alas, time comes and time goes,[9] it subtracts little by little; then it deprives a person of a good, the loss of which he indeed feels, and his pain is great. Alas, and he does not discover that long ago it has already taken away from him the most important thing of all—the capacity to make a resolution—and it has made him so familiar with this condition that there is no consternation over it, the last thing that could help gain new power for renewed resolution!

V
209

No, the saying means very much in earnest, yes, everything for the duly married couple. But it wants to be understood in earnest. It does not want to visit the bridal couple as an unexpected guest who graces the wedding day with his lofty presence, but it desires to settle down with the couple; it wants to be given the test of time, wants to guarantee everything. This is how it wants to be understood, and this is also the only way it can be said: it must be said by a beginner, but by the one who begins with the good resolution. [10]The person who grew old

in the faithful service of love, tested as gold and found true—
the noble poet somewhat amorously says of the slip of a girl
that her young soul was tested gold, but time and danger, after
all, are really the test—the venerable one[11] who over the years
won the rich and incorruptible beauty of faithfulness, faithful
to his commitment according to the dictates of his own conscience, faithful with masculine courage and feminine tender-
ness, with masculine fortitude and feminine sympathy, with
composure of understanding in inwardness of heart, offers the
gentle, friendly, humble counsel of old age: My children, love
conquers everything. And he stirs the young people—alas,
yes, he almost deceives them, because, when he says it, it seems
so easy and the young people would like to hear him say it
again. But if the young people take the saying in vain and light-
mindedly and want to weave a wedding wreath from it, then
experience of the struggles in life steps between the young
people and the venerable one, saying, "Step aside, veneration
for the venerable, first come to know the difficulties"—and
then experience points to him and says, "See here, love has
conquered everything!"

How beautiful to be an old man; compared with such a
witness, what is all eloquence but deceit! Has conquered everything! This is the final word, and it is indeed different and
separate from the first. Oh, stop, you who are passing by, and
consider this difference. When you grasp it, you will indeed
become one who makes a resolution! Has conquered—yes,
this is what experience of struggles in life says with veneration
of the one who has completed his service, whom the covenant
of marriage called to the good fight, whose life leaves no irregularity because he, having loved much,[12] became no one's
debtor. In civil life, of course, when someone wants to travel to
a foreign country and is in debt to someone, his adversary
applies to the authorities who administer justice, and his journey is halted. Ah, if the commitment to a sacred covenant is left
unfulfilled or dubiously fulfilled, is this not like an objection
that makes the last journey into a swindler's flight—but no,
what is the use of fleeing the justice that, judging, watches over
existence—no one escapes that.

Therefore *has* conquered everything! But the saying declares: Love conquers everything. This is how it ought to sound at the beginning and be duly said by the one making the resolution. But the person who is ignorant of the danger, who excludes the danger and does not include an actual conception of it in the resolution, whose courage therefore has lost the victory, just as good deeds miss the reward because the victory[13] has been enjoyed in advance—that person is not resolved. Neither is that person resolved who runs aimlessly[14] and definitely misses the mark because he believes he is near it. Neither is that person resolved who improvidently and relying on an enigmatic power ventures out on the road and does not include in his resolution an actual conception of God's help, of the necessity for it and of its sufficiency. Neither is it a joint resolution, because at that very moment the two are of one mind and both are without resolution.

Does life reveal only one kind of unhappy love in marriage, when death separates and the sorrowing one is left alone? Ah, but death does not have this power to create unhappiness; if nothing else separates them, they are united! However, someone perhaps says, "I know very well what you mean and what the discourse is aiming at, but such things happen only to those who have never been in love; the one who actually loves does conquer everything." It is undeniable, of course, that the person who actually loves does as the saying declares, but does it follow that the one speaking even has a clear conception of what it is actually to love and of life and of the others? A clear conception of what change takes place in the lover when he is actually to conquer everything and this everything is to be actual? What a difference between youthfully wanting to change the whole world and then discovering that it is oneself who must be changed and that the requirement is that this is to inspire, or that the task is to keep oneself unchanged while, alas, everything changed! What a difference between being in the surprise of novelty as the first inventor of everything and then, when laboriousness comes, to discover that it is the monotonous repetition of what has been experienced thousands and thousands of times by the others! What a difference be-

tween youthfully wanting to struggle and the explanation that
there must be suffering and that this is what is to inspire! Wanting to conquer, well, one scales down, thus is willing to fall
before a superior force, but with the consciousness of being the
stronger compared with the individuals—and now the explanation that it is one's own weakness that one must struggle
with, and the requirement, not sympathizing and deploring
but cruel, that one is to be inspired by this struggle! Then when
the huge requirement of the imagined task does not provide the
imagined power, but in actuality it is the insignificant, disdained task; when one is not defying a world that betrayed
one's expectation but sits abandoned by one's great expectation
regarding oneself and robbed of every excuse; when no vast
prospect tempts one to want to venture but one sits idle, discouraged by the paltry task of patience, which becomes even
poorer because time is wasted on wanting to dream youth's
dream all over again—yes, then there is the opportunity to
show that one actually loves or, rather, that the occasion has
waited much too long and that it should not have come to this;
and if the beginning had commenced with a resolution, then
one would have understood in time that it can come to such a
pass.

Look at the one who does indeed resemble the lover—look
at the enthusiast! Does life show only one instance of half-
finished work, of interrupted plans, of a sad and miserable
outcome of a brilliant beginning; is this the one and only instance, that the striving person is prevented by death from
finishing the work, from executing the plan, from reaching the
goal? O death, you are, for all that, powerless; do you really
presume to want to mock an enthusiast! No, the brief unhappiness of the moment of death is soon over, and the one who
dares truthfully to say, "It was death that prevented me," truly
does die with honor, indeed, has gloriously completed his task!
"But," perhaps the young enthusiast, that is, every young enthusiast, says, "I know very well what you are suggesting; you
do not even need to name it; I do not wish to be frustrated and
delayed and discouraged." But this does not happen with the
real enthusiast. That is indeed undeniable, but does the one

v
211

speaking therefore have even a clear conception of what it is to be actually inspired, what it means when it is no longer a matter of leaping like a lion but of remaining on the spot and despite all effort seeming not to move from the spot; when it is not a matter of crossing the whole world in easy flight but of enduring a dead calm in which the enthusiasm will expire; when it is a matter of perceiving the powerlessness and yet not relinquishing the enthusiasm, of hoping against hope;[15] when it is a matter of the long, tedious work that is inseparable from any and every enthusiastic undertaking; when the abandoned one must defend himself even against a sympathy that is the downfall of enthusiasm, although it seems so comforting, and he may be misjudged because he does it; when it is not a matter of reckless impulse but of putting on a straitjacket and of being enthusiastic in it—yes, then there is an opportunity to show that one is actually inspired. And if one has begun with a resolution, it will certainly become apparent what benefit there is in it, because with the resolution one did not take in an invigorating breath of youth but a mistrust of oneself that at a distance knows about the danger.

The first condition for a resolution is to have, that is, to *will* to have a *true conception of life and of oneself.* What is here sown with tears is harvested with songs of joy,[16] and one does recover from the sorrow because the first loss is the best, and the first pain is the one that saves, and the rigorous upbringing is the beneficial one, and the early discipline the strengthening one, and the shudder of the resolution gives courage, and the trembling of the resolution toughens one, and the chastisement of the resolution makes one attentive, and to conquer in the end is the main issue, and the final honor is the only true one!

Ah, death has no power to set up lamentable signs along marriage's road through life. Yet these signs are there. What, then, do they mean? In the customs of a people, there is many a quaint practice connected with a wedding, many a teasing jest that still has its significance, many a roguish prank that is not without beauty, but would it not also be an agreeable practice for the bridal couple, before going to the house where the wedding reception is being held, to go to the house of sorrow, that is, to the earnest consideration from which one does not obtain the bridal veil but the resolution. Let the bride, then, come to the altar in all her loveliness, let the crown of myrtle adorn the beloved—yet it is only the humility of the resolution that makes her pleasing in the eyes of God, and only the actual conception of the resolution makes her strong in holy weakness—to conquer everything.

It is not the purpose of the discourse, even if it were capable of it, to want to terrify with shocking descriptions, to want to evoke dread—to which only the earnest person, when he speaks with authority, can give the sure effect of earnestness and prevent discouragement and dejection, indeed, almost aversion, from interfering with the impression. Ah, are the divorced the only separated married people for whom the binding covenant has become a curse. Are they alone unworthy of the married state who made a wretched beginning by regarding the covenant as a secular arrangement for earthly gain and ended as they began or for whom the marriage tie did not become a deliverance but a trap that incited the sensual desires. Was he alone a bad husband who cravenly and in an unmanly way adoringly wooed a woman's beauty and then in a servile spirit cravenly ruled over a slave, to whose loveliness he in jealousy was a slave—until he ended with the ingratitude of a villain because the years had taken away the youth and beauty of the one to whom he was wedded?

V
213

Ah, no, here it goes as with death in life. Not only those are death's plunder who lie on the sickbed and whom the physician has given up; many whom death has marked walk around among us. Likewise there is among us many a marriage that divorce has marked. See, it has not come between the married couple, but an indifferent exclusiveness separates and alienates each from the other—and yet (and this is why we speak of it), and yet perhaps their old feelings have not become completely extinct. There is no strife between the married couple, no hostile unsettled accounts, but feeling seems to have withdrawn from their life together. Yet they perhaps love each other but await an event that will tighten the bow of resolution and lure forth feeling to expression, inasmuch as the everyday life is not

enough; before each other they are almost ashamed [17]of this
sequence of trifles. They perhaps long for an understanding but
cannot really speak with each other precisely because there is an
opportunity every day; as a consequence, the opportunity is
not used and it becomes more difficult to become open to each
other. They were once so happy—oh, so happy—and this
consciousness that ought to strengthen them, that at least
ought to be always clear, weakens them. They lose the desire
and courage to venture, and that vanished happiness acquires
an exaggerated unhealthy glamor for the two lonely people.
Time goes so slowly; a whole life lies before them. They are
afraid to make the first confession to each other that could unite
them in powerful resolution. Boredom takes the place of unity,
and yet they shun a divorce as a sin, but life is so long. Then the
thought of death sneaks in, because death, after all, dissolves all
bonds. One hardly dares to admit it, and yet it is so, one wishes
oneself dead, as if this were not unfaithfulness—and yet they
perhaps love each other and death perhaps would bring them to
sense this. Then the one seeks the flaw in the other, and instead
of an honest exchange, misunderstanding transacts its sorry
business and estranges each from the other in suspicion and
mistrust, through ungentleness and impatience, and through
flash reconciliations that nourish the sickness, although they
perhaps still love each other.

Was it always poverty and straitened circumstances and life's
adversities that caused this? Ah, a marriage is sometimes maintained in wealth and abundance when the brief honeymoon[18] is
over, in all abundance although on bread and water! —Was it
always only sorrow over wayward children that ultimately
estranged the parents? Ah, how often we see that rare good
fortune in this regard was of no help to the parents. —Was it
always the years that brought this sorrow along? Ah, how brief
a period was sometimes needed before this change had already
occurred. —Was it always an original misrelation in age, in
education, in social class, that sooner or later was bound to
create misunderstanding? Ah, sometimes the two were so perfectly well suited to each other that all they lacked was gratitude in order to be happy. —Was it always environment and

family relationships and connections that corrupted a marriage well begun? Alas, what is the use of placing the blame on others—the weed of corruption has the characteristic that all weeds have: it sows itself. The good seed requires care and work, and if that is lacking the good seed perishes—and then the weeds come by themselves.

Now let the observer who includes himself, who in a critical moment calls forth these thoughts, let him put the question to himself: Do I dare to say that all these married people did not at one time begin with what is called "really being in love with each other," so that they felt the sweetness of surprise when love awakened, felt the restlessness of longing, found time to disappear when they were together and time to be so long when they were apart, found themselves glowing at the thought of wanting to be everything for each other. Let him put the question to himself: Do I dare to deny that the sorry outcome may also have its basis in this, that in the time of youth and hope and surprise and rashness one lacked the direction or earnestness to renounce sentimentality and the lure of the moment and the illusion of fancy in order to subject oneself to the rigorous upbringing of resolution.

What, indeed, does it want, this resolution that is the rebirth of erotic love [*Elskov*]? Does it want to stifle the joy because it wants to save it? Is its solicitude a false friendship because it perhaps is not immediately understood? Is it sheer pain because its beginning is not without pain? Is it perpetual imprisonment because it binds two lovers together in earnest and forever? But its beginning is not without pain and not without a shudder. Think of an enthusiast. Filled with noble intentions, he wants to accomplish so very much, but look at him; in the work of the resolution, the conception of life and of his own weakness so overwhelms him that he sinks in powerlessness, and only the conception of duty holds him in the work in order to win the resolution. What a change! Now he is struggling, weary under the rigorous supervision of duty. Every day he does the little assigned to him, but to the letter as duty bids, and he is still enthusiastic inasmuch as he realizes that whether it is little or much, when duty bids it, it is always much. See, now it succeeds, and the resolution is won, and the work is begun with the genuine criterion. See, it succeeds, and work progresses; see, it succeeds and succeeds beyond expectation, and that first enthusiasm awakens to a renewed and stronger life. See, his enthusiasm was not a rash intention or a perpetual rashness. Neither was it ablaze in youth, then dimly burning in adulthood, and like a smoking candlewick in the evening of life. No, that first enthusiasm went out, as it were, in the night when the resolution came into existence, but then he gained a new enthusiasm and the blessed surprise of wonder from year to year, even in the evening of life. In the same way, through the rigorous upbringing of the resolution, marriage will take away the romantic fancies and illusions and provide a secure abode for erotic love within the impregnable fortress of duty and give the resolved one new enthusiasm and in the course of time daily wonder over his happiness.

[19]But perhaps someone says, "It is insulting to speak to lovers this way, enviously and depressingly to throw suspicion on that happiness instead of admiring and eulogizing, yes, and regarding erotic love's rare happiness with respect." Well, to want to show respect for a rare happiness, be it ever so rare, seems frivolous in an upbuilding meditation that is not assigned to find upbuilding in the divisiveness of happiness in this life. Would not that objection be an outburst of erotic love's seductive persuasiveness, this dangerous power that fosters rashness in the listener?

[20]We are willing to show respect to the poet's rare gift if he uses it well, but the erotic love that inspires the poet to song, is it always to be found like that in life and in every couple united by the covenant of marriage? After all, the poet himself says that it is rare, and the poet's happy gift is in turn a rarity like that erotic love: a supreme wish for a more perfect existence—but no, rather a most beautiful dream arising from a less perfect view of life. That is why the poet explains nothing. He seeks that recollected rarity in the sadness of song; he seeks it flaming in the craving of the wish; he fervently plucks the strings to its honor, as if it were found; he sits weak in the whispering of longing; with the power of his imagination he creates in

thought what is sought. We praise him, and a nation is appropriately proud when it is proud of outstanding poets. But the poet cannot help us ordinary people, because he cannot tell us how to act in order to become the rarity. Therein is the poet's sorrow. The poet is not a proud and haughty man, but his soul has stretched into the infinite; and when he must say to the single individual or of the single individual, "No, he is not that," or "She was not that," he does not wish to insult; himself distressed, he seeks the consolation of song. Therefore we must not be angry with the poet; he loves existence and perhaps feels the pain most because that single individual was not the rarity. Yet no one, says the poet, can provide himself with that rarity; it is an original, and therein is the marvelousness.

v
216

Now, if that rare person existed and one wanted to speak to him about what this discourse is reflecting upon, he would not understand it at all, nor would he respond as that objection responded, because no discourse can disturb an originality such as that. But a deceptive echo of a poetic song, a poor repetition of a poetic work—that can be disturbing. The person, however, who feels within himself that he is not the rare one is indeed concerned. He is not disturbed because the discourse reminds him of his concern—instead he seeks what is upbuilding in the godly meditation. The discourse will go no further than this in order to remove such an objection. But now, my listener, consider the marriage ceremony yourself. Who is performing it? Is it a poet? No, it is someone authorized. [21]The marriage ceremony places everything under sin, and the authorized one conveys the earnestness of it to the single individual and places under sin every person bound by it. Would it then be insulting if the discourse reminded us of the importance of the resolution and that only the resolved person dares to say at the beginning that love conquers everything. To me it seems insulting to assume of anyone that he has not considered this. [22]Even the happiest earthly love needs the resolution's rebirth, needs the rigorous discourse of the marriage ceremony, needs the marriage ceremony's strengthening for the struggle, needs the marriage ceremony's blessing upon the way.

Therefore, in seeking to clarify the holy resolution of marriage, the discourse certainly has reminded you, my listener, of what you yourself have often thought, because the discourse is far from being didactic. You are, then, in agreement with it, and yet you perhaps say, "The discourse is right, but much earnestness is required for such a discourse to produce the right impression, lest it foster impatience or disturb in dejection." You are certainly correct that it requires much earnestness. [23]Indeed, to be a good reader or a good listener is just as great as to be a good speaker, and it is very great when, as here, the discourse is imperfect and without authority. Was not this what you meant, because in making that objection you of course did not want to shove guilt upon the speaker, as if you gained something by accusing him? Let us consider this a bit more closely. Just as a true conception of life is required for making a resolution, so also a true conception of oneself—something implied in what was said—is required. There may have been someone who sent out his spying thoughts to get diversified impressions of life but who could not take himself back, who abandoned himself—and, alas, lost himself. But the person who by marriage binds another person's life to his own, who by marriage makes a commitment that no time will dissolve and every day will require to be fulfilled, from that person a resolution is required, and in this resolution, therefore, a true conception of oneself. And this true conception of oneself, the inwardness of this conception, this is the earnestness.

V
217

Now, just as it is true that in everyone's soul there is a longing like that erotic love the poets celebrate, so there is also in everyone a longing, a wish, that craves what might be called a guide and teacher in life, the tested person whom one can trust, the wise person who knows how to counsel, the noble person who encourages by his own example, the gifted person who has the power of eloquence and the substance of conviction, the earnest person who safeguards the appropriation. [24]For a child it is so easy. One is free from the burden of choice; yes, even if a father were not what he ought to be, the respect the child has, the unconditional obedience, helps it at times to learn the good even from such a father. But then comes the time of youth and of freedom, the time when he, along with his beloved, seeks a guide like that. The point, then, is that freedom and choice are not to become a snare. The sought-after guide of that longing is a rarity. Sometimes he is not even found in every generation, and although you are contemporary with such an eminent person, someone to whom you dare to give yourself entirely, he may not be in the same place as you are, or he was there but must leave it, or you must leave it—and then, yes, then you have to be satisfied with less—that is, you must see to taking care of yourself.

[25]There is confusion enough in life. The most diverse things are proclaimed and recommended and disdained and repeated; the most diverse prototypes appear and disappoint and reappear; the most diverse guidance is offered, and there are always fellow travelers; consolations and evasions and cheers and warnings and victory songs and lamentation are all heard in a confused jumble. Alas, erotic love and marriage are, of course, something in which everyone is tested and about which everyone, therefore, has an opinion and indeed can in truth have if he earnestly wishes to. Everyone, also the unmarried, ought to have an abiding place, and yet there perhaps is many a marriage that does not have it but is tossed about by every breeze. Misled by a chance experience, the young man may think that when external circumstances of affluence and fortunate living conditions favor erotic love it is safeguarded, and he perhaps does not consider how the latitude that his states of mind acquired in that way can foster his difficulties. One person has an exaggerated idea of the complicated task of the spiritual care of a person in love and cannot stoop to the simple task of making a living. Someone else becomes too absorbed in his brimming-over feelings and distaste follows. One of the partners still has some composure and wants to use it, but the other partner misinterprets it and thinks it is coldness and indifference. One partner wishes to economize and be frugal, and the other one does not understand it and thinks it is lack of a sense for something higher. One person is despondent because the repetition around him makes him bored with what he has. Someone else's first happiness makes him impatient; now he compares,

now he recalls, now he suffers a loss. Indeed, who could ever finish naming everything; no discourse is able to do so, and it makes no difference, after all. But no human being can do it, and that is the terrible thing; only one power is able to do it, and that is the resolution, which sees to it in time.

Where, then, is earnestness learned? In life. Most certainly, and the God-pleasing state of marriage indeed provides a rare opportunity. So earnestness is learned—if one takes the resolution along and within it a true conception of oneself. The resolution itself is the earnestness. In order to learn earnestness from what is called the earnestness of life, earnestness is already presupposed. [26]The earnestness of life is not like a schoolteacher in relation to the learner, but in a certain sense is like an indifferent power in relation to the person who must himself be something of a teacher in relation to himself as the learner. Otherwise one can learn indifference to everything even from the earnestness of life. One does indeed wish for guidance, and yet also in this connection it holds true that one must have earnestness oneself in order to be helped by the guidance. Or has it not happened that even when that rare guide stood among us, we hit upon all kinds of things to weaken his influence, as if he himself lost thereby and not we ourselves, as if it were the wisdom of the years to become more and more fastidious, more and more proficient in rejecting, instead of becoming more and more discerning.

And now if there is no such person, what then? Well, the world never seems to be short of guides. See, now one person wants to guide everyone and cannot help himself; then another is hailed as wise, and admiration recognizes him by his not even being able to understand what the simple person understands. Now someone has the power of persuasion and leads astray, has the powerful works of falsehood; now what one learned in childhood is supposed to be obsolete and one has to learn all over again. Now someone wants to tear the husband from his wife's side and make him important through his participation in great enterprises, wants to teach him to look down on the sacred calling of marriage; now someone tempts the wife and teaches her to sigh under the yoke of marriage. Now they want to dangle before the husband and wife a joint effort in achievements that make the marriage relationship unimportant; now they want to teach married people enjoyment, want to take their children from them and at the same time their cares so that the parents are able to live for higher pursuits. Then an expectation of something extraordinary is intensified, a new order of things that is coming, and we all, both the married and the unmarried, get a vacation, like schoolchildren, because the schoolteacher is going to move, have a vacation until he gets settled again—but we are not schoolchildren any longer, and everyone must make his own accounting to God, and marriage's sacred commitment will indeed assign its task and its responsibility every day.

[27]So where does a person find guidance if he himself does not work out his own soul's salvation in fear and trembling;[28] then he does indeed become earnest. Otherwise it will turn out that he cannot follow the one guide, because even though he means so well he still is weak; and he cannot follow the other one, because, as people say, although he has power and pith in what he says, he does not mean it; or the one is too old to satisfy the times, and the other is too young. Yes, how would a discourse ever come to an end if it were to describe this confusion in life. But what do you think, my listener, of the kind of person who certainly had the appearance of earnestness in rejecting everything but not a trace of its power in possessing the least thing; what do you think of such a one if he were a married man and thus had become married without resolution and therefore went on living unconcerned about the most sacred commitment, that is, without earnestly caring about it. Has not divorce put its mark also on that kind of marriage, a marriage in which the married couple indeed belong to each other but not in earnest!

No, the earnestness is within a person, and only a dupe chases after it, and only a coward buys the indulgence of mediocrity by being as most people are and scouting around for it, and only the timorous one is disturbed in a more noble striving by paying attention to the opinion of others. If there is no guide in life, the earnest person still does not walk in the dark. Ah, my listener, even if the appointed guide in the place where you live were incompetent, well, if you so choose, be the good listener who still benefits from his mediocre discourse. And if the person speaking here is perhaps too young or perhaps expresses himself unclearly or his thought is unclear—well, my listener, then put the discourse aside or, if you choose, do the great thing, be the good reader who benefits even from an inadequate discourse. As a matter of fact, just as there is supposed to be a power of discourse that can almost work miracles, so there is also a listener's power that can work miracles if the listener so chooses. That kind of listener is the earnest listener. He says, "I want to be built up," and so he is built up.

But the earnestness lies in a resolution. If anyone is afraid of it, no wonder that he seeks consolation in others' being trapped in the same difficulty and scouts to the right and to the left. If anyone thinks that a resolution is a fragile thing and that the person who has made a resolution is skating on thin ice—well, no wonder, then, that he must always have a lot of people around him in order to find the courage to live. But you, my listener, you do indeed think that the resolution is the highest blessedness, that even if erotic love's richest happiness could in any way be guaranteed to you for your whole life, you would still choose the dangers of the life of resolution and marital life together. The resolution performs the miracle at weddings just like that at the wedding in Cana.[29] It offers the poor wine first and keeps the best for last; erotic love is the beloved's best adornment, but the resolution is a power in the heart of the imperfect one. The resolution of marriage is that love [*Kjærlighed*] conquers everything. Yes, it conquers everything, but it does perish in adversity if no resolution holds it firm, it perishes in prosperity if no resolution holds it firm, it degenerates in the everyday if no resolution encourages it, it is stifled in imagined importance if no resolution humbles it. Erotic love remains, but the resolution is its abiding place, whereby it has its continuance; erotic love is the refreshing volatile element, but the resolution is the vessel in which it is sustained. Erotic love remains; it guides through life when the resolution accompanies it, but it goes astray when the resolution does not guide;

it gives life meaning when the resolution interprets it day after day; it suffices for a whole life when the resolution exercises a restraining influence; it grasps the eternal when a resolution has prepared a place there; it conquers everything when the resolution accompanies it on the day of battle—and the final honor is the one and only honor.

Is this discourse envious? Is it envious to say to the happy person, "I know where you should hide your happiness in order to keep it secure"? A little flattering sadness, which of course would simply be envy, might titillate the senses of a happy person. Is this discourse insulting? Is it insulting to say to someone, "I am convinced that you yourself know and have considered this matter, and therefore I only remind you of it"? Is the speaker obtrusive who stands apart and speaks rather softly with himself?

[30]So, then, a true conception of life and of oneself is required for the resolution of marriage; but this already implies the second great requirement, which is just like the first: *a true conception of God*. The one entirely corresponds to the other, because no one can have a true conception of God without having a corresponding conception of life and of oneself, or a true conception of oneself without a corresponding conception of God, or a true conception of life without a corresponding conception of oneself. A poetic creative fancy, or a conception at the distance of indifferent thought, is not a true conception. Neither does the conception of God come as an incidental addendum to that conception of life and of oneself. On the contrary, it comes and penetrates and crowns everything and was present before it became clear.

The lovers are certainly happy, and on the day of happiness one is surely closest to God. But a true conception of God is required; an understanding between God and the happy one is required, and thus a language is required in which they talk with each other. This language is the resolution, the only language in which God will involve himself with a human being. Even if the happy one were ever so enthusiastic in his expressions of thanksgiving for his happiness (and where, indeed, would there be a happy person who did not feel this need to be

V
221

thankful!), and even if he mentioned God's name, it would not follow that he spoke with God, had a true conception of him, made himself understood to him, and had the benefit of the understanding. The thanksgiving for the happiness, however exceptional it is, however deeply emotional the expression, however fervent the soul, God will not understand—only the resolution that takes over the happiness. Even if God's name is mentioned first and last, one still is not speaking with God if the conception in which the worshiper expresses his thanks is not of God but of happiness, fate, the great prize, and the like, or of an enigmatic power, whose intervention prompts one to be amazed—and to idolize.

The resolution certainly should not make the happy one ungrateful; on the contrary, it should make him worthy, and the earnestness of thankfulness is only in the resolution. Therefore the resolution's thanksgiving is conscious that this happiness is a task, and that the person giving thanks is now standing at the beginning. Therefore the resolution's thanksgiving is thoughtful; it understands that in the happiness God has spoken to the resolved person, but also understands that this is the beginning of the conversation.

Is this thinking poorly of the happiness? Is it not rather thinking worthily of God! If someone spoke with a wise person and then, immediately upon hearing the wise person's first words, which shed the light of truth in his soul, interrupted him with his thanksgiving because now he needed no more help, what else would this show except that he was not speaking with a wise person but with a wise person whom he himself transformed into a fool? Now, a wise person is a human being, and as such also something external; to that extent someone may indeed truthfully say, even though he spoke foolishly, that he had spoken with a wise person. But God is only in the internal. Therefore the one who speaks with him as that man spoke with the wise person does not actually speak with him. Just as there is an immature love that says, "The real lover conquers everything," yet without having a true conception of the struggle, and just as there is an immature enthusiasm that says the same thing with similar rashness—so also there is an immature thanksgiving that wants to thank God and yet only deceives itself by thinking that it is thanking God and defrauds God of the thanksgiving.

The resolution's thanksgiving is earnest and therefore well pleasing to God; its thanksgiving is also the good beginning by which half is won, and with God the resolution will surely conquer everything. It does not give thanks once and for all, nor with earthly and fraudulent self-conceit or unwisdom. No, the resolution is the beginning, and the resolution's thanksgiving is the beginning of the thanksgiving, the beginning of the solemnity that will hold at bay many a needless danger, give strength in actual danger, echo in the hymn of thanksgiving on the day of victory. It is the beginning of the vigilance that will find the married couple constant in the evening of life, as expectant after the wedding as the wise bridesmaids were before the wedding,[31] the vigilance that will make the final thanksgiving the most beautiful, make the final response to God's speaking, the beginning of which was that happiness, the well-pleasing and true thanksgiving of gratitude.

If anyone thinks that this would be disturbing, would he, without wanting to understand himself properly, muddle-headedly dare to think poorly of God? Would anyone believe that the happiness would be lost by becoming earnest, that the happiness would be depreciated by being the beginning of happiness—would it then be more beautiful, would it be wiser, would it better stand the test in life if there were a beginning without a resolution? Would it be more beautiful if the happiness promptly separated, so to speak, the two who are joined; would it be more beautiful if a vain feminine heart voluptuously heard the praises of an adorer when he believed that he owed everything to her and when, muddleheaded but grateful for his happiness, he did not know anyone else to thank? Or would it be more beautiful if the proud head bowed to hear voluptuously the adoration of someone who is weak, when she, glad in her happiness, humble in gratitude, did not know to whom she should go except to him, to him to whom she indeed owed everything and her happiness—to him who defrauded her of the best? Would it be more beautiful, would it be wiser? Would it stand its test better—also when at some time the yoke had to be cast off and the struggle begin, or if that did not happen, when the poor wretch never did become a man but, devoid of manly courage, went through life tied to a woman's apron strings, or if the pitiable faithful one slaved life away, not as a wife, but abjectly loved her master, and this master was her husband? Or is idolatry initially indeed more beautiful, basically wiser, and as life progresses more reliable than a reasonable worship of God?

If anyone thinks that the resolution's conception of God is a halt from which the happiness would rather be excused—would it then be more beautiful, would it be wiser, would it better stand the test in life if the two, without the resolution, rushed away with each other in the transitory moment of infatuation's dream, if they danced away the soundness and health of love on the wedding day? Would it be more beautiful, would it be wiser, would it bear up better in life—also when they wearily stood at the beginning of the road, and behold, the fun was over, and behold, it was not earnestness that remained but loathing and boredom and a confused awakening from a confused youthful dream to a long life ahead—would the brief pleasure of a couple of idol-worshipers actually be more beautiful and wiser and more reliable in life than the humble beginning of a true marriage?

Does anyone think that the resolution can come later, when it is really needed? Then it is not yet needed, not on the wedding day, when the eternal commitment is made? But then later? Would he think that there is no thought of abandoning each other but of enjoying the first delight of the union—and then, united, to support each other by means of the resolution? So when trouble and hardship come, and distress, whether earthly or spiritual, stands at the door—then that is the time? Yes, indeed, then that is the time—for the resolved one to collect himself in his resolution, but it is definitely not the time to put together a resolution. It is true that distress and adversity can help a person to seek God in a resolution, but the question is whether the conception is always the right one, whether it is joyful, whether it does not have a certain wretchedness, a secret wish that it not be needed, whether it is not harmful or envious or depressed and therefore is no ennobled rendering of the adversities of life. There is a government loan office where the poor can go. The indigent person is helped, but do the poor have a joyful conception of this loan office? Likewise, there perhaps are marriages that seek God only in adversity, alas, and seek him as a loan office; and anyone who only then seeks him always runs this danger. Would such a late resolution, which even though worthy is still not bought at the last moment without shame and without great danger—would it be more beautiful and wiser than the first resolution of marriage?

V
224

But perhaps no distress and no adversity at all comes in life, and then of course the resolution is not needed. Far be it from the aim of the discourse to terrify childish people, and even further to recommend the resolution as a means that is supposed to serve something inferior. So, then, you childish one who does not want to become acquainted with spiritual dangers, so things are going well. See, here is a marriage that life pampers and good fortune smiles upon unceasingly—what then? Then this childish marriage has still lost the very best, because the resolution itself is the glorious thing. It is not a wretched invention against the wretchedness of life but is the garment of salvation, and the resolved one is adorned with it to bear worthily the days of prosperity, and the resolved one is powerfully armed in it to conquer on the evil day, and yet the attire is the same.

Alas, how utterly different married life and marriage conditions are in this world, and yet there is one resolution common to each and every one or can be so: that love [*Kjerlighed*] conquers everything. This resolution is the beginning, and in this resolution is contained a true conception of life and of oneself and hence of God—then the end indeed becomes like the beginning: that love has conquered everything.

But think of two marriages, my listener. The one must laboriously make its hard way through many adversities; the other is carried through life as if on the hands of good fortune. Now they have both arrived at the boundary of life, and love has conquered everything. Of the first marriage it may be said that the married couple learned much from the rigorous school of life, but when it also may be said that in the evening of life they still had not become essentially different in their earnestness than when they in the beginning won earnestness in the rigorous upbringing of the resolution—would this not be very beautiful? And if it may be said of the other couple that in the evening of life the married people were not essentially different in earnestness but throughout their long life had been essentially just as earnest as on that happy day when the resolution matured them in earnestness—would this not be very beautiful? The resolution's earnestness of youth is not formed piecemeal but is formed by God from the conception of life and of oneself and of God and therefore is an eternal healthiness and perhaps is never gained in this way later.

V
225

# At a Graveside[1]

Then all is over! —And when the person stepped up to the grave first because he was the next of kin, and when after the brief moment of the speech he was the last one at the grave, alas, because he was the next of kin—then all is over. If he remained out there, he still would not learn what the deceased is doing, because the deceased is a quiet man; if in his trouble he called out his name, if in his grief he sat listening, he still would learn nothing, because in the grave there is quiet, and the deceased is a silent man; and if recollecting[2] he visited the grave every day, the one dead would not recollect him—.

In the grave there is no recollection, not even of God.[3] See, the man did know this, the one of whom it must now be said that he no longer recollects anything, to whom it would now be too late to say this. But because he knew this, he acted accordingly, and therefore *he recollected God* while he was living. His life was passed in honorable obscurity; not many were aware of his existence; among those few only one or two knew him. He was a citizen of the town here; a hard worker in his modest occupation, he disturbed no one by disregarding his civic obligations, disturbed no one by misplaced concern about the whole. So it went year after year, uniformly but not emptily. He grew up, he grew old, he became aged—his work was and remained the same, the same occupation in the different periods of his life. He leaves behind a wife, happy to have been united with him in the past, now an old woman who grieves for the lost one, a true widow who, forsaken, has her hope in God. He leaves behind a son who learned to love him and to find contentment in his situation and his father's work. At one time as a child joyful in his father's house, as a youth he never found it too cramped; now it is a house of mourning for him.

Not many inquiries are made about the death of such an obscure man, and if anyone shortly thereafter walks past the house where he lived in lowliness and reads his name over the door, because the little business is continued under his name, it will indeed seem as if he were not dead. Just as he slept gently and peacefully away, so in the surrounding world his death is a departure in silence. Respectable as a citizen, honest in his business, thrifty in his household, charitable according to his means, sincerely sympathetic, faithful to his wife, a father to his son—all this and all the truth with which this can be said do not raise expectations for a momentous ending; here it is a life's activity to which a quiet death became a beautiful ending.

Yet he still had one more work; in simplicity of heart it was performed with the same faithfulness: he recollected God. He was a man, old, he became aged, and then he died, but the recollection of God remained the same, a guide in all his activity, a quiet joy in his devout contemplation. Indeed, if there were no one at all who missed him in death, yes, if he were not with God now, God would miss him in life and know his dwelling and seek him there, because the deceased walked before him[4] and was better known by him than by anyone else. He recollected God and became proficient in his work; he recollected God and became joyful in his work and joyful in his life; he recollected God and became happy in his modest home with his dear ones; he disturbed no one by indifference to public worship, disturbed no one by untimely zeal, but God's house was to him a second home—and now he has gone home.

But in the grave there is no recollection—therefore it remains behind, remains with the two who were dear to him in life: they will recollect him. And now when the person who stepped up to the grave first because he was the next of kin and after the brief moment of the speech was the last one at the grave because he was the next of kin, when he, recollecting, departs, he goes home to the sorrowing widow—and the name over the door becomes a recollection. Now and then for a time there will come a customer who casually or more solicitously asks about the man, and when he hears of his death the customer will say, "Well, so he is dead." When all the old customers have done that once, the life of the locality has no longer any means of preserving the recollection of him. But the old widow will need no reminder in order to recollect, and the busy son will not find it a hindrance to recollect. When no one asks about him anymore, then the name over the door—when the house is no longer visibly a house of sorrow, when also the

V
228

grief in the house has abated and the daily loss has with consolation practiced recollection—then the name over the door will
signify to the two that they also have one additional work: to
recollect the one who is dead.

Now the speech is over. Just one act remains—with the three
spadefuls of earth to commit the deceased, like everything that
has come from the earth, to earth again—and then all is over.

The unauthorized discourse cannot carry this out in earnest as
here described; there is no death waiting for it so that all can be
over. But despite this, you, my listener, can pay heed to the
discourse. Death itself certainly has its own earnestness. The
earnestness lies not in the event, not in the external situation
that now another person has died, no more than the difference
in earnestness lies in the number of carriages, indeed, no more
than the mitigated mood that only wants to speak well of the
dead is earnestness or could in the remotest way satisfy the
person who thought earnestly about his own death. Death can
expressly teach that earnestness lies in the inner being, in
thought, can teach that it is only an illusion when the external is
regarded light-mindedly or heavy-mindedly or when the observer, profoundly considering the thought of death, forgets to
think about and take into account his own death. [5]If someone
wants to name a proper object of earnestness, one names death
and "the earnest thought of death,"[6] and yet it seems as if there
is a jest underlying death, and this jest, varied in dissimilarity of
mood and expression, is essential to every contemplation of
death in which the contemplator himself is not alone with
death and does not think of himself and death at the same time.
A pagan has already declared that one ought not to fear death,
because "when it is, I am not, and when I am, it is not."[7] This is
the jest by which the cunning contemplator places himself on
the outside; but even if the contemplation of death uses pictures
of horror to describe death and terrifies a sick imagination, it is
still only a jest if he merely contemplates death and not himself
in death, if he thinks of it as the human condition but not as his
own. The jest is that this unyielding power cannot, as it were,

get at its victim, that there is a contradiction, that death, as it were, tricks itself.

[8]Sorrow—if you wish to compare it to death and want to call sorrow an archer, as death is—sorrow does not miss its mark, because it hits the living, and when it has hit him, only then does the sorrow begin; but when death's arrow has hit, then indeed it is over. And sickness, if you want to compare it to death and if you want to call sickness a snare, as death certainly is a snare in which life is caught—sickness actually does catch, and when it has caught the healthy the sickness begins. But when death tightens the snare it has indeed caught nothing, because then all is over.

But the earnestness lies in just this, and just this differentiates the earnestness of death from the earnestness of life, which so easily allows one to deceive oneself. When someone goes his way bowed low in adversity, sufferings, sickness, lack of appreciation, hardship, and wretched prospects, he draws the wrong conclusion if on the basis of that he directly concludes that he is earnest, because earnestness is not the direct version but the ennobled one—that is, here again it is the inner being and the thinking and the appropriation and the ennobling that are the earnestness.

If someone is occupied in a complex undertaking, perhaps is in command of many soldiers, perhaps writes many books, perhaps holds high positions; if one perhaps has many children, or frequently must be in mortal danger, or has the sober job of dressing corpses, he draws the wrong conclusion if on the basis of that he straightway concludes that he is earnest—because earnestness is in the impact; earnestness is the earnestness of the inner being, not of the job. In this sense, however, death is not something actual, and as soon as one is dead it is too late to become earnest. If someone meets sudden death, something a more earnest age regarded as the greatest misfortune (which is why it is mentioned in the ancient prayer[9]) but which a later age regards as the greatest good fortune, then one is indeed helped. Life's earnestness is earnest, and yet there is no earnestness unless the external is ennobled in one's consciousness; in this lies the possibility of illusion. The earnestness of death is without deception, because it is not death that is earnest but the thought of death.

Therefore if you, my listener, will fix your attention on this thought and concern yourself in no other way with the consideration than to think about yourself, then this unauthorized discourse will become an earnest matter also with you. To think of oneself as dead is earnestness; to be a witness to the death of another is mood. There is the light touch of sadness when the passerby is a father who carries his child for the last time, carries it to the grave; or when the indigent hearse drives by and you know nothing about the dead person except that he was a human being. There is a sadness when youth and health become death's booty, when many years later the image of the beautiful one appears on the crumbling monument on the grave, surrounded by weeds; there is an earnestness in mood when death intrudes into the vain pursuits and snatches the foolish girl dressed in her most vainglorious finery, snatches the fool in his most vainglorious moment; there is a sigh over life's mockery when the dead person had made the certain promise and without fault became a deceiver, because he had merely forgotten that death is the only certainty; there is a longing for the eternal when death took and took again and now took the last outstanding person you knew; there is a fever heat or cold fire of soul illness when someone becomes so familiar with death and the loss of next of kin that life becomes soul-destroying for him; there is sheer sorrow when the dead person was one of yours; there are the labor pains of immortal hope when it was your beloved; there is the jolting breakthrough of earnestness when it was your one and only guide and loneliness overwhelms you—but even if it was your child, even if it was your beloved, and even if it was your one and only guide, this is still a mood; and even if you would willingly die in their place, this also is a mood, and even if you think that this is easier, this also is a mood. Earnestness is that you think death,[10] and that you are thinking it as your [11]lot, and that you are then doing what death is indeed unable to do—namely, that you are and death also is.

Death is the schoolmaster of earnestness, but in turn its ear-

V
230

nest instruction is recognized precisely by its leaving to the single individual the task of searching himself so it can then teach him earnestness as it can be learned only by the person himself. Death minds its own business in life; it does not run around, as the timorous think, and sharpen its scythe and scare women and children—as if this were earnestness. No, death says, "I exist; if anyone wants to learn from me, then let him come to me." Only in this way does death occupy one in earnestness—otherwise only in mood through the ingenuity of thought, through its profundity, or jestingly in elated fancy, or bowing in deep sorrow that in its most suffering expression still is not earnestness, because earnestness would expressly teach one to be moderate in sorrow and lamentation.

[12]A poet has told of a youth who on the night when the year changes dreamed of being an old man, and as an old man in his dream he looked back over a wasted life, until he woke in anxiety New Year's morning not only to a new year but to a new life.[13] Likewise, to be wide awake and to think death, to think what surely is more decisive than old age, which of course also has its time, to think that all was over, that everything was lost along with life, in order then to win everything in life—this is earnestness. There was an emperor who had himself buried in accordance with all the formal customs.[14] His action was perhaps only a mood, but to witness his own death, to witness the closing of the casket, to witness that everything that fills the senses in a worldly and mortal way ceases in death—this is earnestness. To die is indeed the lot of every human being and thus is a very mediocre art, but to be able to die well is indeed the highest wisdom of life. Wherein lies the difference? In this, that in the one case the earnestness is the earnestness of death, in the other it is the earnestness of the mortal being. And the discourse that makes the distinction cannot, of course, address itself to the dead but to the living.

The discourse will therefore be about:

## death's decision.

We surely do agree, my listener, that a godly discourse ought never be divisive or be at odds with anything except what is ungodly. For example, when the poor man, the servant who must use sparingly the few hours of his infrequent time off, goes to visit a grave in order to recollect someone who is dead and also to think about his own death, when someone like that has to make the most of his meager opportunities, the walk out there also becomes a pleasure, the visit out there also becomes a joyful and salutary diversion from the many days of work—so that the time out there is spent now in remembering the one dead, now in thinking earnestly about himself, and now in being delighted with his freedom and the surroundings, as if one were seeking recreation in a beautiful region, as if the walk were only for pleasure and thus food was brought along for combined delight. We surely do agree that in his noble simplicity such a person beautifully unites contradictions (which, according to the words of the wise, is the ultimate difficulty), that his recollecting is precious to the deceased, is received with joy in heaven, and that his earnestness is just as laudable, just as well-pleasing to God, just as serviceable to him as that of someone who with rare talent used day and night in [15]practicing in his life the earnest thought of death, so that he was halted and halted again in order to renounce vain pursuits, was prompted and prompted again to hasten on the road of the good, now was weaned of being talkative and busy in life in order to learn wisdom in silence, now learned not to shudder at phantoms and human inventions but at the responsibility of death, now learned not to fear those who kill the body[16] but to fear for himself and fear having his life in vanity, in the moment, in imagination. We laud him for so magnificently using the opportunity granted him; if, however, he occasionally took time off from this magnificent daily task in order to be entertained by the thought that he was better than the simple person who had neither such time nor such talents more pleasing to God, as if God were utterly unjust and denied the time and talent to the one, that is, the gift of good fortune, and then in turn, as people sometimes in thoughtlessness act cruelly, made the lack of them a guilt—alas, what a difference between his rare time off and the simple man's time off, when he forfeits everything and the simple man gains everything! No, all comparison is only a jest and a conceited comparison a dismal jest.

Even if that favored one had plenty of time, earnestness and death would still teach him that he had no time to waste [*spilde*] and even less to forfeit [*forspilde*] everything. If, however, someone were speedily to finish with the thought of death just as with all other thoughts and perhaps haughtily worried that there would not be enough in this poor and monotonous life for such a speedy thinker to think about, then we surely do agree, my listener, that it is the characteristic of every object when it becomes an object of godly contemplation that the simple person is quickly helped to a beneficial understanding and that the most gifted person gladly uses a whole lifetime, even if he admits that he has neither completely understood it nor perfectly practiced the thought in his life. The person who is without God in the world[17] soon becomes bored with himself—and expresses this haughtily by being bored with all life, but the person who is in fellowship with God indeed lives with the one whose presence gives infinite significance to even the most insignificant.

[18]Concerning death's decision, the first thing to be said is that it is *decisive*. The repetition of the word is significant, and the repetition itself reminds us of how sparing of words death is. There is many another decision in life, but only one is decisive the way death's decision is. All the forces of life are incapable of resisting time; it sweeps them along with itself— even recollection is in the present. [19]One who is living does not have it in his power to stop time, to find rest outside time in the perfect conclusion, in a conclusion of joy as if there were no tomorrow, in a conclusion of sorrow as if it could not be a drop more bitter, in a conclusion of the contemplation as if meaning were entirely finished and the contemplation were not in turn a part of the meaning, in the conclusion of accounting as if the moment of settling an account did not also take on its own responsibility. Death, however, has this power; it does not dabble with the decision as if there were still a little left over; it does not chase after the decision as the living person does—it carries it out in earnest. [20]When death comes, the word is: Up to here, not one step further;[21] then it is concluded, not a letter is added; the meaning is at an end and not one more sound is to

be heard—all is over. [22]If it is impossible to unite all the sayings of the countless living in one saying about life, all the dead are united in one saying, in one single saying to the living: Stand still. If it is impossible to unite all the sayings of the countless living in one saying about the endeavors of their lives, all the dead are united in one, in one single saying: Now all is over.

See, death is able to do this. [23]But it is no inexperienced youth who has not learned to use the scythe, so that someone would be able to dumbfound him. Have any notion you wish, fanciful or true, about your life, about its importance for everybody, about its importance for yourself—death has no notion and pays no attention to notions.[24] [25]Ah, if anyone ought to be tired of repetition, death certainly ought to be, which has seen everything and the same thing again and again. It has seen many times even the death uncommon for centuries; yet no dying person has ever seen death change color, has seen it shaken by the sight, has seen the scythe tremble in its hand, has seen a hint of a change of countenance in its calm face. Neither has death now become an old man who, debilitated by age, gropes around vaguely, does not exactly know what time it is, or has become compassionate out of weakness. Ah, if anyone dares to compliment himself on being unchanged, death certainly does—[26]it does not become paler or older.

But the discourse is not to eulogize death, no more than it will occupy the imagination. That death can make a finish is indeed certain, but the challenge of earnestness to the living is to think it, to think that all is over, that there comes a time when all is over. This is the difficult thing, because even in the moment of death the dying person thinks that he still might have some time to live, and one is even afraid to tell him that all is over. And now the living, as long as he is living perhaps in health, in youth, in happiness, in power—that is, safeguarded, yes, well safeguarded if he is not willing to shut himself in with the thought of death, which explains to him that this security is false. There is a consolation in life, a false flatterer; there is a safeguard in life, a hypocritical deceiver—it is called postponement. But it is seldom called by its proper name, because even when one wants to say it, it insinuates itself into the word and the name becomes somewhat toned down, and of course the toned-down name is also a postponement. On the other hand, there is no one who can teach us to loathe the flatterer and to see through the deceiver as the earnest thought of death can. Death and postponement are irreconcilable and they are mortal enemies, but the earnest person knows that death is the stronger.

So all is over. If it was a child with a claim to an entire life, if it wept for itself—all is over now, not a moment is conceded. If it was a youth with his beautiful hopes, if he pleaded for himself, for just one single hope—all is over now, not a penny is paid to him for his claim to life. If a little was lacking of a man's renowned work, and if this work was a wonder of the world and all humankind would misunderstand it because the conclusion was lacking—all is over now, the work is not completely finished. If it was a single word that had been the meaning of his life and if he would give a whole life to dare to say it—all is over now, the word was not said.

So by death's decision all is over; there is rest. Nothing, nothing disturbs the dead. If that little word or that lacking moment made the death struggle agitated, now the dead one is not disturbed; if the suppression of that little word disturbed the lives of many of the living, if that enigmatic work engaged the researcher again and again, the dead one is not disturbed. Death's decision is like a night, the night that comes when one cannot work;[27] indeed death has been called a night, and the conception has been mitigated by calling it a sleep. It is supposed to be mitigating for the living one when, sleepless, he futilely seeks rest on his bed at night, when, fleeing from himself, he futilely seeks a hiding place where consciousness cannot discover him, when the tormented one, weary in body and soul from intense suffering, futilely seeks a position in which there is relief, when he cannot stand still because of the pain and cannot walk because of exhaustion, until he collapses and then in a new effort futilely seeks a restful position, futilely seeks coolness in this heat. It is supposed to be mitigating to think that there is still one position in which the exhausted one finds rest. It is the position of death, one bed on which he rests quietly, the bed of death; one sleep that does not run away, the sleep of death; one cool place, the grave; one hiding place where consciousness stands outside, the grave, where recollec- V 235 tion itself remains outside like a light breeze in the trees; one quilt the quiet man cannot throw off, under which he sleeps quietly, the quilt of green grass! It is supposed to be mitigating, if in youth one has already grown weary and sadness wants to nurse the child, then to consider that in the womb of the earth one lies comfortably; it is supposed to be so mitigating to consider this consolation and to think of it in this way, that the eternal finally becomes the unfortunate one who, like a night nurse, does not dare to sleep while all the rest of us fall asleep!

But, my listener, this is a mood, and to think about death in this way is not earnestness. To long for death in this way is depression's escape from life, and in this way to be unwilling to fear death is rebellion. It is the fraudulence of sadness to be unwilling to understand that there is something else to fear than life, and therefore a consoling wisdom other than the sleep of death must be found. Truly, if it is weak to fear death, then it is a prinked-up courage that fancies itself not afraid of death when the same person fears life; it is an indulgent lethargy that wants to go to bed—that is, indulgently wants to sleep itself into consolation, indulgently wants to sleep itself away from suffering.

Yes, admittedly death is a sleep, and thus we want to say that everyone resting in death is sleeping, we want to say that a silent night is shading the dead and that nothing disturbs their peace. But is there no difference between life and death? The living person who is thinking about his own death views it otherwise. What if you yourself, you were the living one, who saw it! Look at the one who is sleeping in death; he is not flushed like a child in sleep; he is not gathering new strength like the man who is being reinvigorated; the dream is not paying him a visit in friendliness the way it visits the old man in his sleep! When you see someone who looks more dead than alive, what do you do? You call to the person who has fainted because this condition makes you shudder—that is, when the condition of death is that of a living person; is it comforting, then, that the reason you do not call to the dead person is that it cannot help! But you are indeed not dead, and if depression wants to brace you by means of an epileptic seizure, [28] if sadness wants to make you faint in deathly exhaustion that finds its only consolation in the sleep of death, then call out, then shout to yourself; do for yourself what you would do for anyone else and do not seek deceptive comfort in wishing all was over! Whatever the fanciful or true conception you have of the singularity of your suffering—ah, if anyone must be weary of the repetition of the mournful scream, death certainly must be; even the unfortunate one for centuries unmatched in suffering, even his mournful scream death has heard many times, but no one, no one has hinted that it moved death to come more swiftly! Even if your scream could move him—is that really your intention, or is it not rather the contradiction, that he does not come because you call, that fortifies the egotism of defiance; is it not the contradiction that helps the timorous ones play the brave game with the terror. If, then, your scream and your longing did move him, are you not deceiving yourself even if we were to forget momentarily the responsibility that always remains? What was it that gave relief; was it this, that all was over, or was it not the idea of this, as this was still in the power of depression and sadness and in the power of a living person—a diversion, a plaything! See, the person who sleeps in death does not move, and even if the coffin clothes are not too tight he still does not move; he becomes dust. The thought that all is over, which in the idea's most fanciful advance payment depressingly refreshed him in defiant weakness or flirtatiously soothed him in sadness, that thought is not present in him. Therefore he has no joy in its being over—why, then, did he desire it so much? What a contradiction! Say then that it is so comforting to rot in the ground. But if you know something else about death, you also know how to fear something else than life.

Earnestness certainly understands the same about death but understands it differently. It understands that all is over. Whether this, mitigated in mood, can be expressed by saying that death is a night, a sleep, is of minor concern to it. Earnestness does not waste much time in guessing riddles; it does not sit sunk in contemplation, does not rewrite expressions, does not think about the ingeniousness of imagery, does not discuss, but acts.

If it is certain that death exists, which it is; if it is certain that with death's decision all is over; if it is certain that death itself never becomes involved in giving any explanation—well, then it is a matter of understanding oneself, and the earnest understanding is that if death is night then life is day, that if no work can be done at night then work can be done during the day; and the terse but impelling cry of earnestness, like death's terse cry, is: This very day.

Death in earnest gives life force as nothing else does; it makes one alert as nothing else does. Death induces the sensual person to say: Let us eat and drink, because tomorrow we shall die[29]— but this is sensuality's cowardly lust for life, that contemptible order of things where one lives in order to eat and drink instead of eating and drinking in order to live. The idea of death may induce weakness in the more profound person so that he sinks relaxed in mood, but the thought of death gives the earnest person the right momentum in life and the right goal toward which he directs his momentum. No bowstring can be tightened in such a way and is able to give the arrow such momentum the way the thought of death is able to accelerate the living when earnestness stretches the thought. Then earnestness grasps the present this very day, disdains no task as too insignificant, rejects no time as too short, works with all its might even though it is willing to smile at itself if this effort is said to be merit before God, in weakness is willing to understand that a human being is nothing at all and that one who works with all one's might gains only the proper opportunity to wonder at God.

V
237

Indeed, time [*Tid*] also is a good. If a person were able to produce a scarcity [*Dyrtid*] in the external world, yes, then he would be busy. The merchant is correct in saying that the commodity certainly has its price, but the price still depends very much on the advantageous circumstances at the time— and when there is scarcity, the merchant profits. A person is perhaps not able to do this in the external world, but in the world of spirit everyone is able to do it. Death itself produces a scarcity of time [*Dyrtid paa Tid*] for the dying. Who has not hear' how one day, sometimes one hour, was jacked up in price when the dying one bargained with death! Who has not heard how one day, sometimes one hour, gained infinite worth because death made time dear! Death is able to do this, but with the thought of death the earnest person is able to create a scarcity so that the year and the day receive infinite worth—and when it is a time of scarcity the merchant profits by using time. But if public security is unsettled, the merchant does not carelessly pile up his profits but watches over his treasure lest a thief break in and take it away from him; alas, death also is like a thief in the night.[30]

Is this not true, my listener; and have you yourself not experienced this? And when the thought of death visited you but made you inactive, when it sneaked in and beguiled your life force into romantic dreaming, when death's despondency would make your life a vanity, when that seducer, sadness, prowled around you, when the idea that all was over would anesthetize you into the sleep of depression, when you lost yourself in absentminded preoccupation with the symbols of death—then you did not lay the blame on death, because all this was indeed not death. But you said to yourself, "My soul is in a mood, and if it continues this way, then there is in it a hostility toward me that can gain domination." Then you did not flee death, as if that would be the cure. Far from it. You said, "I will summon the earnest thought of death." And it helped you, because the earnestness of death has helped to make a final hour infinitely meaningful; the earnest thought of it has helped to make a long life as meaningful as in a time of scarcity, as watchful as if sought by thieving hands.

So, then, let death keep its power, "that all is over," but let life also keep the right to work while it is day;[31] and let the earnest person seek the thought of death as an aid in that work. The vacillating person is only a witness to the continual boundary struggle between life and death, his life only doubt's statement of the situation, the ending of his life an illusion, but the earnest person has made friends with the contenders and in the earnest thought of death he has the most faithful ally. Even though the equality of all the dead is that now all is over, there is still one difference, my listener, a difference that cries aloud to heaven—the difference of what that life was that now in death is over. So all is not over, and despite all death's terror—no, supported by the earnest thought of death, the earnest person says, "All is not over." But if this bright prospect is tempting, if he once again merely glimpses it in the half-light of contemplation, if it puts distance between him and the task, if time does not become a scarcity, if the possession of it is secure for him— then again he is not earnest. If death says, "Perhaps this very day," then earnestness says, "Let it perhaps be today or not," but I say, "This very day."

[32]Concerning death's decision, the next thing that must be said is that it is *indefinable*. By this nothing is said, but this is the way it must be when the question is about an enigma. Death does indeed make all equal, but if this equality is in nothing, in annihilation, then the equality is itself indefinable. If there is to be further discussion of this equality, it can be done only by citing life's dissimilarity and denying this in regard to death's equality. Here in the grave the infant and the person who transformed a world are equally inactive; here the rich man is just as poor as the poor man; here poverty does not beg, the rich man has nothing to give, and the most contented person and the most insatiable person need just as little; here the voice of the ruler is not heard, nor the cry of the oppressed; here the arrogant and the injured are equally powerless. Here they lie, grave by grave, and tolerate one another, those whom enmity separated by a whole world; here lies the beautiful one and here the wretched one, but beauty does not separate them; here they both lie, the one who was on the lookout for death as for a hidden treasure, and the one who had forgotten that death existed, but the difference is undetectable.

Because of its equality, death's decision is like an empty space and like a silence in which nothing is heard, or it is toned down like a silence that is not disturbed. And in this silent kingdom, death is the ruler. Although one against all the living, it is still powerful enough to make them his subjects and to command silence. Whatever conception you want to have of your life, yes, even of its significance for the eternal, you do not talk yourself out of death, you do not make the transition to the eternal in the course of a speech and with one breath—they have all been obliged to be silent. Even if generation noisily united with generation in one common task and if the single individual forgot himself and found himself very secure under the cover of the crowd—behold, death takes each one separately—and he becomes silent. Whatever difference you want to imagine in the one living, death makes him just like the person whose dissimilarity did not make him distinguishable. To the vain person, the mirror of life sometimes depicts his dissimilarity with flattering faithfulness, but the mirror of death does not flatter; its faithfulness shows all to be identical; they all look alike when death with its mirror has demonstrated that the dead person is silent.

[33]Death's decision is therefore not definable by equality, because the equality consists in annihilation. And pondering this is supposed to be alleviating for the living! When the spirit, weary of dissimilarity, which goes on and on and never ends, proudly withdraws into itself and in the defiance of powerlessness accumulates anger over its inability to check the life force of dissimilarity—then it is supposed to be alleviating to consider that death has this power, then this conception is supposed to fan that enthusiasm of annihilation into a glow in which there is supposed to be heightened life. —When the poor wretch sighs in his corner because life, like a stepmother, has done him wrong, when he, so deformed he does not even dare to show himself because even the best of people involuntarily smile at his excruciating, alas, and yet ludicrous misery, when he, cut off in this way, does not love because in him no one finds a match, which he is futilely seeking in others—then it is supposed to be as alleviating as the cooling of snow for the hidden fire of resentment to consider that death makes all equal! —When someone violated smarts under the injustice of the powerful and in powerlessness the hate despairs of revenge—then it is supposed to be a welcome consolation that almost restores the joy of life to think that death makes all of

them equal. —When the pampered wishful thinker sits idle and flirts with his wishes' great ideas of himself but only sees that others strive and achieve great things, when he can scarcely breathe because of his furious impatience—then it is supposed to be alleviating, it is supposed to give air, to consider that death crosses out everything and makes all equal. —When the loser realized that now the struggle was over and that he was the weaker one, but also realizes that all is not over yet, that his defeat gave the momentum of good fortune to the victor, that his suffering is every day in consequence of the defeat but the report of the other's ascent at a distance is more and more remote—then it is supposed to be mitigating to consider that death will fetch him and make the separation into a nothing! — When sickness becomes a daily visitor and time passes, the time of joy, and even those closest become weary of the suffering one and many an impatient word wounds, when the sufferer himself feels that his mere presence is disturbing to the joyful, and so he must sit far away from the dance—then it is supposed to be a relief to reflect that death invites him also to the dance, and in that dance all become equal.

V
240

But, my listener, this is a mood; and actually it is cowardice, which by a counterfeit, clad in poetic form, wants to think itself superior, although in essence it still is just as paltry. If the simple person is perhaps not able to grasp this kind of mood, is this exclusiveness in itself a decisive value, is it not decisive only in making the mood more responsible? It is a cowardly craving of depression to want to become dizzy in the emptiness and to seek the final diversion in this dizziness; it is envy in rebellion against God to want to damage one's soul,[34] wounded by dissimilarity; it is self-denunciation in powerlessness to want to hate; it betrays that one simply lacks power when one makes dreadful use of powerlessness. It is a contemptible shortcut to a groundless complaint against life for someone merely to wish and then to complain against life because he did not become what he wished and never becomes proficient in anything but wishing and finally becomes wretched enough to wish everything away. It is self-tormenting doggedness for the vanquished to refuse to under-

stand anything higher than the conflict between you and me
and the downfall of both; it is a still more terrible sickness to
refuse to comprehend which physician the sick one needs.
Truly, if it is cowardly and voluptuous pampering not to dare
even in thought to relinquish the advantageous dissimilarity
and having one's life wrapped up in it, then it is a prinked-up
courage that wants to experiment with the idea of death's
equality when the same person sighs or gasps under life's
dissimilarity.

If it actually were anyone's idea to want to be consoled in this
way by the equality of death—would it not be the contradiction of continuing to live that would give the presumptuous
daring deed its allure? Did his conception of death prove true in
death, that is, when the intellectual pursuit no longer entertained his passion? The dead one has, of course, forgotten the
dissimilarity; and even if he was determined to recollect it all
his life in order to have the pleasure of seeing it taken away
from someone else in death, this thought is certainly not with
him in death, even if we momentarily want to forget the responsibility that awaits. This is the lie and the deception in the
presumptuous defiance that wants to conspire with death
against life. It is forgotten that death is the strongest; it is forgotten that it has no preferences, that it does not make a pact
with anyone, so that in death he acquires a free pass and latitude
for the enjoyment of being annihilated. Only when the living
person's conception of death roams around in fantasy in the
silent kingdom of the dead, itself playing that it is death, and
vanishes in death; only when the living person's conception
impersonates death, summons the person it envies, divests him
of all his glory and delights in his powerlessness; only when the
conception goes out to the graves, presumptuously shoves the
spade into the ground, violates the peace of the dead by its
defiant desire that the remains of one dead individual look
exactly like another's[35]—only then is there relief.

But all this is not earnestness; however dark its nature and
however somber the attraction, that still does not make it earnestness. Earnestness does not scowl but is reconciled with life
and knows how to fear death.

Earnestness, then, understands the same thing about death but understands it in a different way. It understands that death makes all equal, and this it has already understood, because earnestness has taught it to seek before God the equality in which all are able to be equal. In this endeavor the earnest person discovers a dissimilarity, namely, his own dissimilarity from the goal that is assigned to him, and discovers that a condition most distant from this goal would be like the equality of death. But every time earthly dissimilarity wants to tempt, wants to delay, the earnest thought about the equality of death intervenes and again impels.

Just as no evil spirit dares name the holy name, so every good spirit shudders before the empty space, before the equality of annihilation, and [36]this shudder that is productive in the life of nature is impelling in the life of spirit. Ah, how often, when death came to a person, the equality of annihilation taught him to wish the most oppressive dissimilarity back again, taught him [37]to find the terms desirable now when the terms of death were the only ones! In this way the earnest thought of death has taught the living person to permeate the most oppressive dissimilarity with the equality before God. [38]No comparison has that impelling power and so reliably gives the urgent person the true direction as does the comparison the living person makes between himself and the equality of death. If the most conceited of all comparisons is the one made when a person disdains all other comparisons in order to compare himself with himself in self-satisfaction; indeed, if perhaps no vain woman ever stood so vain, surrounded by admiration, as when she stood alone before her mirror—ah, then no comparison is as earnest as the comparison of the one who, alone, compares himself with the equality of death. Alone, because that is indeed what death makes him when the grave is closed, when the cemetery gate is shut, when night falls and he lies alone, far away from all sympathy, unrecognizable in the shape that can only evoke a shudder, alone out there where the multitude of the dead do not form any kind of society. Behold, death has been able to overthrow thrones and principalities, but the earnest thought of death has done something just as great; it has

helped the earnest person to subordinate the most advantageous dissimilarity to the humble equality before God and
has helped him to raise himself above the most oppressive
dissimilarity into the humble equality before God.

Is it not true, my listener, have you not experienced something like this yourself? When your soul went astray in preferential treatment and you could scarcely recognize yourself for
all the glory, the earnest thought of the equality of death made
you unrecognizable in another way and you learned to know
yourself and to want to be known before God. Or if your soul
sighed under the severe limitations of suffering, adversity, insults, and depression and, alas, it seemed to you as if the limitations would last a lifetime, then when the tempter also came to
your house (you know him, the tempter one has in one's own
inner being and who deceptively brings greetings from others)
and when he at first dangled before you the good fortune of
others until you became dejected and he then wanted to give
you compensation—then you did not surrender to mood. You
said, "It is rebellion against God, enmity against myself"; and
then you said, "I will summon the earnest thought of death."
And it helped you to surmount the dissimilarity, to find the
equality before God and to want to express this equality. The
equality of death is terrifying because nothing can withstand it
(how disconsolate!), but the godly equality is blessed because
nothing can prevent it unless the person himself wills to do so.
Would life's dissimilarity be so great then!

Take the joyful one, let him rejoice in his good fortune—if
you, the unfortunate one, were joyful again over his good
fortune, would you not then both be joyful? Take the person of
distinction, let him delight in his advantages—if you, the in-
sulted one, had forgotten the affront and now saw his excel-
lence, would the difference indeed be great? Take the youth, let
him hurry on with the confidence of hope—if you, although
disappointed by life, perhaps even assisted him secretly, would
the difference then be so great? Ah, good fortune and honor
and wealth and beauty and power—these do indeed constitute
the dissimilarity. But if the only difference is that one person's
good fortune and honor and wealth and beauty and power are a

field plant and the other's a grave flower that is cultivated in the sacred soil of self-denial—is the difference then so great; after all, they are both fortunate and honored and rich and beautiful and powerful. Alas, no, then a person needs no compensation, least of all the kind that deceitfully suppresses the fact that he himself becomes nothing. However oppressive the dissimilarity was, the earnest thought about the equality of death, like the strict upbringing, did help to renounce worldly comparison, to understand annihilation as something even more terrible, and to want to seek the equality before God.

The equality of death was not permitted to enchant you with its sorcery—after all, there is no time for that either. Just as death's decision is *not definable* by *equality*, so it is likewise *not definable* by inequality. Who has not frequently heard it said that death makes no distinctions, that it recognizes neither status nor age. Who has not himself often pondered that when he named the most varied circumstances of a living person and then wanted to think of death in relation to them, the conclusion was that death could just as well seek its booty here as there, just as well, because in death no consideration is shown, whereas all dissimilarity involves showing consideration. So death is not definable by its inequality. It almost steals a march on life, and the baby is born dead; it lets the old man wait year after year. When someone says peace and security,[39] death stands over him, and in mortal danger death is sometimes sought futilely, while it finds the person who is hiding in an out-of-the-way place. When the barns are full and there are provisions for a long life, death comes and demands the rich man's soul;[40] when there is want, it stays away. When the hungry person worries about what he will have to eat tomorrow,[41] death comes and takes away from him his worry about making a living; when the sated voluptuary worries about what he will have to eat tomorrow, death comes in judgment and makes his worry superfluous.

So death is indefinable—the only certainty, and the only thing about which nothing is certain. This conception lures thought out into the shifting of the indefinable in order to try its hand at this shuddering as in a game, in order to guess at this amazing enigma, in order to indulge in the inexplicable disappearance and the inexplicable eruption of the sudden.[42] It is supposed to be mitigating to think about this coincidence, this like and unlike, this law intimated in the lawless, which is and is not, which stands in relation to everything living and which is indefinable in every one of its relations.

When the soul becomes weary of compulsion and constraint, of the definable and of the meager daily measure of the definable task and of the consciousness that more and more is being neglected; when the power of the will has served its time and the enervated one has become just like dry-rot wood; when curiosity, weary of life, seeks a more diverse task for its curiosity—then it is supposed to be entertaining to consider the indefinability of death and in a mitigating way to become familiar with that thought. Now one is surprised at a particular death, now at another; now one talks oneself giddy by talking in general terms about what eludes general definition; now one is in one mood, now in another, now sad, now undaunted, now mocking, now connecting death to the happiest moment as the greatest good fortune, now as the greatest misfortune, now wishing for a sudden death, now a slow one; now one [43]is made weary in the discussion about which death is the most desirable, now one becomes bored with the whole deliberation, forgets death, until the wheel of contemplation is again set in motion and shakes the details of the contemplation into new patterns for new amazement—alas, yes, until the thought of one's own death evaporates in a fog before the eyes and the reminder of one's own death becomes an indefinite buzzing in the ears. This is the mitigation of familiarity in the dulled one's view that for better or for worse this is the way it is, in the elevating impersonal forgetfulness that forgets itself over the whole or, rather, forgets itself in thoughtlessness, whereby one's own death becomes a droll instance in all these manifold unpredictable instances, and the ending of one's time of service becomes a preparation that makes the transition of one's own death easy.

But even if a life such as this experienced all possible moods by contemplating the singularity of death, is the contemplation therefore earnestness? Does the prolixity of moods always end in earnestness; should not the commencement of earnestness rather be the prevention of that prolixity in which the contemplator neglects his life and becomes like the person addicted to gambling when he ponders and ponders and dreams about numbers in the night instead of working during the day.[44] The person who views death in this way is in a drugged condition with regard to his spiritual life; he weakens his consciousness so it cannot endure the earnest impression of the inexplicable, so he cannot in earnestness submit to the impression but then also represses the enigmatic.

V
245

Yes, death certainly is a singular enigma, but only earnestness can define it. Indeed, from what does that confusion of thoughtlessness come but from this, that the individual's thought ventures, observing, out into life, wants to survey the whole of existence, that play of forces that only God in heaven can view calmly, because in his providence he governs it with wise and omnipresent purpose, but which weakens a human being's mind and makes him mentally deranged, causes him misplaced care, and strengthens with regrettable consolation. Misplaced care, namely in mood, because he worries about so much; regrettable consolation, namely in slack lethargy, when his contemplation has so many entrances and exits that it eventually wanders. And when death comes, it still deceives the contemplator, because all his contemplation did not come a single step closer to the explanation but only deceived him out of life.

Earnestness, then, understands the same thing about death, that it is indefinable by inequality, that no age or circumstance or life situation is a safeguard against it, but thereupon the earnest person understands it in another way and understands himself. See, the axe already lies at the root of the tree; every tree that does not bear good fruit will be cut down[45]—no, every tree will be cut down, also the one that bears good fruit. The certainty is that the axe lies at the root of the tree. Even if you do not notice that death is passing over your grave and that the axe is in motion, the uncertainty is still there at every moment, the uncertainty when the blow falls—and the tree.

But when it has fallen, then it is decided whether the tree bore good fruit or rotten fruit.

The earnest person looks at himself. If he is young, the thought of death teaches him that a young person will become its booty here if it comes today, but he does not dally in ordinary talk about youth as death's booty. The earnest person looks at himself; so he knows the nature of the one who would become death's booty here if it were to come today; he looks at his own work and so he knows what work it is that would be interrupted here if death were to come today. Thus the game ends, [46]the enigma is solved. The ordinary view of death only confuses thought, just as wanting to experience in general does. The certainty of death is the earnestness; its uncertainty is the instruction, the practice of earnestness. The earnest person is the one who through uncertainty is brought up to earnestness by virtue of certainty.

V
246

How does a person learn earnestness? Is it by having an earnest person dictate something to him so that he can learn it? Not at all. If you have not yourself learned in this way from an earnest man, then imagine how it goes. See, the learner concerns himself (without concern there is no learner) about some object with his whole soul, and in this way the certainty of death becomes an object of concern. Now the concerned person turns to the teacher of earnestness, and thus death is indeed not a monster except for the imagination. The learner now wants this or that; he wants to do it thus and so and under these assumptions—"And it is bound to succeed, is it not so?" But the earnest person answers nothing at all, and finally he says, yet without mockery but with the calmness of earnestness, "Yes, it is possible!" The learner already becomes a little impatient; he suggests a new plan, changes the assumptions, and concludes his speech in a still more urgent way. But the earnest person is silent, looks calmly at him, and finally says, "Yes, it is possible!" Now the learner becomes passionate; he resorts to pleas or, if he is so equipped, to clever locutions—indeed, he perhaps even insults the earnest person and becomes totally confused himself and everything around him seems to be confusion. But when with these weapons and in this condition he charges at the earnest person, he has to endure his unaltered calm gaze and put up with his silence, because the earnest person merely looks at him and finally says, "Yes, it is possible."

This is the way it is with death. The certainty is the unchanging, and the uncertainty is the brief statement: It is possible. Every condition that wants to make the certainty of death into a conditional certainty for the wisher, every agreement that wants to make the certainty of death into a conditional certainty for the person making up his mind, every arrangement that wants to condition the certainty of death as to time and hour for the one who is acting, every condition, every agreement, every arrangement runs aground on this statement; and all passionateness and all cleverness and all defiance are rendered powerless by this statement—until the learner sees the error of his ways. But the earnestness lies in just this, and it was to this that certainty and uncertainty wanted to help the learner. If certainty is allowed to leave open the question of what it can be, like a universal caption over life, instead of being like the endorsement of the particular and the daily by usage, as happens with the help of uncertainty—then earnestness is not learned. Uncertainty lends a hand and, like the teacher, points steadily to the object of learning and says to the learner, "Pay close attention to the certainty"—then earnestness comes into existence. No teacher is able to teach the pupil to pay attention to what is said the way the uncertainty of death does when it points to the certainty of death; and no teacher is able to keep the pupil's thoughts concentrated on the one object of instruction the way the thought of the uncertainty of death does when it practices the thought of the certainty of death.

V
247

The certainty of death determines the learner once and for all in earnestness, but the uncertainty of death is the daily or at least the frequent or necessary surveillance that watches over the earnestness—only this is earnestness. No supervision is so meticulous, not the father's over the child, not the teacher's over the pupil, indeed, not the warden's over the prisoner; and no surveillance is so ennobling as the uncertainty of death when it examines the use of time and the nature of the work, that of the one making up his mind or of the one acting, that of a youth or of an old man, that of a man or of a woman. With regard to well-spent time in relation to the interruption of death, it is not essential whether the time was long or short; and with regard to the essential work in relation to the interruption of death, it is not essential whether the work was finished or only begun. With regard to the accidental, the length of time is the decisive factor, as with happiness, for example—the end alone decides whether one has been happy.[47] With incidental work, which is in the external, it is essential that the work be finished. But the essential work is not defined essentially by time and the external, insofar as death is the interruption. Earnestness, therefore, becomes the living of each day as if it were the last and also the first in a long life, and the choosing of work that does not depend on whether one is granted a lifetime to complete it well or only a brief time to have begun it well.

[48]Finally, it must be said of death's decision that it is *inexplicable*. That is, whether or not people find an explanation, death itself explains nothing. [49]If you were able to catch sight of him, the pale, grim harvester, where he stood idle, leaning on his scythe, and if you would then go up to him, whether you thought your boredom with life might curry favor with him or that your burning longing for the eternal might move him if you laid your hand on his shoulder and said, "Explain yourself, just one word"—do you think he would reply? I think he would not even notice that you put your hand on his shoulder and spoke to him. Or if death came, alas, so opportunely, alas, as the greatest benefactor, as a rescuer; if it came and saved a person from incurring the guilt that is not repented in life because the guilt puts an end to life; if the unhappy person were now to thank death for bringing him what was sought and for preventing him from becoming guilty—do you think that death would understand him? I think that death would not hear a word of what he said, because it explains nothing. Whether it comes as the greatest benefaction or the greatest misfortune, whether it is hailed with jubilation or with desperate opposi-

tion, death knows nothing about that, because it is inexplicable. Death is the transition; it knows nothing about the circumstances, nothing at all.

See, this inexplicableness certainly needs an explanation. But the earnestness lies in just this, that the explanation does not explain death but discloses the state of the explainer's own innermost being. What an earnest warning to be slow to speak![50] Even if one must smile upon seeing thoughtlessness putting its hand in support under the pondering head that is supposed to fathom the explanation, even if one must smile again when this thinker comes out with the explanation; or when, as if it were a universal summons, even the most frivolous thoughts are in passing ready with a notion, a comment, as an explanation, and make use of the rare opportunity, inasmuch as death is indeed an inexplicable enigma for everyone—alas, the judgment earnestness pronounces upon such behavior is that the explainer is informing against himself, is betraying how thoughtless, how poor, his life is. Therefore, reticence about the explanation is already an indication of some earnestness, which at least understands that death, just because it is nothing, is not some sort of strange inscription that every passerby is supposed to try to read or a curiosity that everyone must have seen and have an opinion about. What is decisive about the explanation, what prevents the nothingness of death from annihilating the explanation, is that it acquires retroactive power and actuality in the life of the living person; then death becomes a teacher to him and does not traitorously assist him to a confession that denounces the explainer as a fool.

[51]As the inexplicable, death can indeed seem to be everything and nothing at all, and the explanation seems to be to pronounce this all at once. Such an explanation indicates a life that, satisfied with the present, defends itself against the influence of death by a mood that holds death in the equilibrium of indecisiveness. Death does not acquire power to disturb such a life; it does acquire influence, however, but not the retroactive power to transform such a life. The explanation does not change in the various moods, but at every moment death is placed outside life in the equilibrium of indecisiveness, which

puts it at a distance. To paganism, the highest courage was the wise person (whose earnestness was indicated expressly by his not being in a hurry with the explanation) who was able to live with the thought of death in such a way that he overcame this thought every moment of his life by indecisiveness. Then the earthly life is lived to the end. The wise person knows that death exists; he does not live thoughtlessly, forgetting that it exists. He meets with it in his thoughts, he renders it powerless in indeterminability, and this is his victory over death—but death does not come to penetrate his life and transform it.

As the inexplicable, death might seem to be the supreme good fortune. An explanation such as that betrays a life of childishness; the explanation is like the final fruit of that life: superstition. The person with this explanation had a child's and adolescent's conception of the pleasant and the unpleasant. Life went on, and he found himself deceived; he became older in years but not in mind; he grasped nothing of the eternal. Then the childishness within him concentrated in an exaggerated notion that death would come and bring everything to fulfillment.[52] Death now became the friend sought for, the beloved, the rich benefactor who had everything to give that his childishness had futilely sought to have fulfilled in life. At times this good fortune is spoken of frivolously and recklessly, at times sadly; sometimes the explainer even pushes forward vociferously with his explanation and wants to help others, but the explanation merely betrays the state of the explainer's own inner being, betrays that he did not perceive the retroactive effect of earnestness but is childishly hurrying ahead, childishly pinning his hopes on death as he did on life.

As the inexplicable, death may seem to be the greatest misfortune. But this explanation indicates that the explainer is cowardly clinging to life, perhaps cowardly to its favor, perhaps cowardly to its suffering, so that he fears life but fears death even more. Death does not acquire retroactive power, that is, not by virtue of the conception, because otherwise it is retroactive and makes the favor of good fortune joyless for the one and makes the earthly suffering hopeless for the other.

[53]Then, too, the explanation has used other descriptive

names and has called death a transition, a transformation, a
suffering, a struggle, the last struggle, a punishment, the
wages of sin.[54] Each one of these explanations contains a whole
life-view. What an earnest challenge to the explainer! It is easy
to recite them all by rote, easy to explain death when it costs no
effort to refuse to understand that the discourse is about the
acquiring of retroactive power in life through the explanation.
Why does anyone want to transform death into a mockery of
himself? Death has no need of an explanation and certainly has
never requested any thinker to be of assistance. But the living
need the explanation—and why? In order to live accordingly.

V
250

If someone thinks, for example, that death is a transformation, this may indeed be quite true. But just suppose that the
uncertainty of death, which walks around like a teacher and
watches every moment to see if the pupil is paying attention,
just suppose it discovered that the explainer's interpretation
was something like this: I have a long life ahead of me, thirty
years, yes, perhaps forty, and then death will come sometime
as a transformation[55]—what would the teacher think of this
pupil who had not even grasped the idea of the uncertainty of
death? Or if someone thinks that it is a transformation that will
intervene at some time and death's uncertainty now makes an
inspection and discovers that he, not unlike a gambler, is waiting for death as an event that will happen sometime, what
would the teacher think of this pupil who was not even aware
that in death's decision all is over and that the transformation
cannot fall in line with other events as a new event—because in
death it is finished?

[56]See, one can have an opinion about remote events, about a
natural object, about nature, about scholarly works, about another human being, and so on about much else, and when one
expresses this opinion the wise person can decide whether it is
correct or incorrect. No one, however, troubles the opinion-
holder with a consideration of the other side of the truth,
whether one actually does have the opinion, whether it is just
something one is reciting. Yet this other side is just as important, because not only is that person mad who talks senselessly,
but the person is fully as mad who states a correct opinion if it

has absolutely no significance for him.[57] The one shows the other the confidence, the acknowledgment, of assuming that he means what he says. Alas, yet it is so easy, so very easy, to acquire a true opinion, and yet it is so difficult, so very difficult, to have an opinion and to have it in truth.

Now, inasmuch as death is the object of earnestness, here again earnestness is: that we should not be overhasty in acquiring an opinion with regard to death. In all earnestness the uncertainty of death continually takes the liberty of making an inspection to see whether the opinion-holder actually does have this opinion—that is, makes an inspection to see whether his life expresses it. With regard to something else, one can express an opinion and then if one is required to act by virtue of this opinion, that is, show that one has it, innumerable escapes are possible. But the uncertainty of death is the pupil's rigorous oral examiner, and when the pupil recites the explanation, uncertainty says to him, "Well, now I will make an inquiry as to whether this is your opinion, because now, right now at this moment, all is over, for you all is over; no escape is thinkable, not a letter to be added; so I will find out whether you actually meant what you said about me." Alas, all empty explaining and all verbiage and all embellishing and all concatenating of earlier explanations in order to find an even more clever one, and all the admiration for this and all the trouble with it—all this is merely diversion and absentmindedness in intellectual abstraction—what does the uncertainty of death think about that?

[58]Therefore, the discourse will refrain from any explanation. Just as death is the last of all, so this will be the last thing said about it: It is inexplicable. The inexplicability is the boundary, and the importance of the statement is simply to give the thought of death retroactive power and make it impelling in life, because with the decision of death all is over, and because the uncertainty of death inspects every moment. Therefore, the inexplicability is not a request to solve enigmas, an invitation to be ingenious, but is death's earnest warning to the living: I need no explanation; but bear in mind, you yourself, that with this decision all is over and that this decision can at

V
251

any moment be at hand; see, it is very advisable for you to bear this in mind.

[59]My listener, it perhaps seems to you that you learn very little from this discourse;[60] you perhaps know much more yourself, and yet it may not have been futile if the conception of death's decision has been the occasion to remind you that knowing a great deal is not an unconditional good. Perhaps it seems to you that the thought of death has only become terrifying, and that it still has also a gentler, a more friendly side for consideration, that the weary laborer's longing for rest, the tired traveler's hastening toward the exit, the concerned one's trust in the pain-stilling sleep of death, and the misunderstood person's sad urge to sleep in peace are also a beautiful and legitimate explanation of death. Undeniably! But it is not learned by rote, it is not learned by reading about it, it is acquired slowly, and it is acquired only by the person who worked himself weary in the good work, who walked himself tired on the right road, who bore the concern for a just cause, who was misunderstood in a noble striving, and not until it is well gained in this way is it in the right place and a legitimate discourse in the mouth of the Very Reverend.[61]

V
252

But the youth does not dare to speak this way lest the beautiful explanation, just like the wise saying in the mouth of a fool, become an untruth in his mouth. To be sure, I have heard that a child's and adolescent's earnest teacher later became the mature adult's friend, but I have never heard, at least not from anyone from whom I wished to learn, that it began with the teacher's promptly becoming a playmate or the child's becoming an old man, nor that this friendship in truth commenced then. This is the way it is with the thought of death. If it has never with terror halted the young person's life and used the earnestness only to moderate the terror; if the uncertainty of death has not had its time of instruction in which it taught him with the rigorousness of earnestness—then I have never heard, at least not from anyone whose knowledge I would want to share, I have never heard from such a person that there was any truth in it if someone called death his friend, inasmuch as he had never had him as anything but a playmate, if, already weary of life in his youth, he spoke fraudulently about death's friendship in order to deceive life, if, without having enjoyed life as an old man, he spoke fraudulently about death's friendship in order to deceive himself.

The person who has spoken here is young, still at the age of a learner; he comprehends only the difficulty and the rigorousness of the instruction—oh, would that he might succeed in doing it in such a way that he would become worthy of daring at some time to rejoice in the teacher's friendship! The person who has spoken here is, of course, not your teacher, my listener; he is merely letting you witness, just as he himself is doing, how a person seeks to learn something from the thought of death, that teacher of earnestness who at birth is appointed to everyone for a whole lifetime [62]and who in the uncertainty is always ready to begin the instruction when it is requested. Death does not come because someone calls it (for the weaker one to order the stronger one in that way would be only a jest), but as soon as someone opens the door to uncertainty, the teacher is there, the teacher who will at some time come to give a test and examine the pupil: whether he has wanted to use his instruction or not. And this testing by death—or with a more commonly used foreign word to designate the same thing—this final examination [*Examen*] of life, is equally difficult for all. It is not as it usually is—namely, that the fortunately gifted person passes easily and the poorly gifted person has a hard time—no, death adapts the test to the ability—oh, so very accurately, and the test becomes equally difficult because it is the test of earnestness.

# SUPPLEMENT

# KEY TO REFERENCES

Marginal references alongside the text are to volume and page [V 100] in *Søren Kierkegaards samlede Værker*, I–XIV, edited by A. B. Drachmann, J. L. Heiberg, and H. O. Lange (1 ed., Copenhagen: Gyldendal, 1901–06). The same marginal references are used in Sören Kierkegaard, *Gesammelte Werke*, Abt. 1–36 (Düsseldorf, Cologne: Eugen Diederichs Verlag, 1952–69).

References to Kierkegaard's works in English are to this edition, *Kierkegaard's Writings* [*KW*], I–XXVI (Princeton: Princeton University Press, 1978– ). Specific references to the *Writings* are given by English title and the standard Danish pagination referred to above [*Either/Or*, I, p. 120, *KW* III (*SV* I 100)].

References to the *Papirer* [*Pap.* I A 100; note the differentiating letter A, B, or C, used only in references to the *Papirer*] are to *Søren Kierkegaards Papirer*, I–XI³, edited by P. A. Heiberg, V. Kuhr, and E. Torsting (1 ed., Copenhagen: Gyldendal, 1909–48), and 2 ed., photo-offset with two supplemental volumes, I–XIII, edited by Niels Thulstrup (Copenhagen: Gyldendal, 1968–70), and with index, XIV–XVI (1975–78), edited by N. J. Cappelørn. References to the *Papirer* in English [*JP* II 1500], occasionally amended, are to the volume and serial entry number in *Søren Kierkegaard's Journals and Papers*, I–VI, edited and translated by Howard V. Hong and Edna H. Hong, assisted by Gregor Malantschuk, and index, VII, prepared by Nathaniel J. Hong and Charles M. Barker (Bloomington: Indiana University Press, 1967–78).

References to correspondence are to the serial numbers in *Breve og Aktstykker vedrørende Søren Kierkegaard*, I–II, edited by Niels Thulstrup (Copenhagen: Munksgaard, 1953–54), and to the corresponding serial numbers in *Kierkegaard: Letters and Documents*, translated by Henrik Rosenmeier, *Kierkegaard's Writings*, XXV [*Letters*, Letter 100, *KW* XXV].

References to books in Kierkegaard's own library [*ASKB* 100] are based on the serial numbering system of *Auktionsprotokol over Søren Kierkegaards Bogsamling* [Auction-catalog of Søren Kierkegaard's Book-collection], edited by H. P. Rohde (Copenhagen: Royal Library, 1967).

In the Supplement, references to page and lines in the text are given as: 100:1–10.

In the notes, internal references to the present volume are given as: p. 100.

Three spaced periods indicate an omission by the editors; five spaced periods indicate a hiatus or fragmentariness in the text.

# Tre Taler

ved

# tænkte Leiligheder.

Af

## S. Kierkegaard.

**Kjøbenhavn.**
Hos Universitetsboghandler C. A. Reitzel.
Trykt i Bianco Lunos Bogtrykkeri.
**1845.**

Three Discourses

on

Imagined Occasions.

By

S. Kierkegaard.

Copenhagen.
Available at University Bookseller C. A. Reitzel's.
Printed by Bianco Luno Press.
1845.

# SELECTED ENTRIES FROM
## KIERKEGAARD'S JOURNALS AND PAPERS
## PERTAINING TO
### *THREE DISCOURSES ON IMAGINED OCCASIONS*

There is indeed a shocking eloquence (even though shocking in a different sense than the voice of Abel's blood, which cries out to heaven[1]) when one reads the brief words that a deceased person has had placed over his grave, the last words, his final testament, the last cry, into which he has poured his whole soul. What is all preacher-prattle compared with this commentary. In the lower part of the Helliggeistes Church there are some small basement windows with iron bars. A skull is depicted there, together with a brief inscription. Thus does the grave call out to one. —Death's last struggle, when there is no time anymore to select widely or to chatter about categories or about the difference between paganism and Christianity.—*JP* I 714 (*Pap.* V A 36) *n.d.*, 1844

My reader, it is very curious, but not everyone gets to become an author in this life—for that various talents are required. Ah, but go out into the graveyard and look at the graves and you will see that occasionally someone has become an author without even giving it the slightest thought. Those brief inscriptions, a pious saying, an admonition—for example, remembrance of the God-fearing is a benediction—out there everything preaches; just as nature declares God, so every grave preaches. There is a gravestone with the bust of a young girl. No doubt she was beautiful at one time, and now the stone has sunk and nettles grow over the grave. She seems to have had no family. Here is the grave of a soldier; his helmet and sword lie upon the coffin, and beneath it says that his memory shall never be forgotten. Yet, alas, the top of the railing is already torn down and one is tempted to seize his sword to

V
A 56
23

V
A 56
24

defend him, since he is doing it no longer—and those who
mourned him thought that his memory would never be
forgotten!—*JP* I 715 (*Pap.* V A 56) *n.d.*, 1844

It is clear that the place politics occupied in Greece has been
taken in Christianity by religion (genuine folk Christianity),
which is a subject for discussion and is influenced by discussion. Therefore, in a purely formal way Aristotle's *Rhetoric* will
throw much light on religious issues. The whole question of
being and nonbeing, which is not found at all in Aristotelian
philosophy (his οὐσία πρώτη [primary substance] and δεύ-
τερα [secondary], see *Categories*,[2] are something else entirely),
he transfers to rhetoric as that which is supposed to produce
conviction. πίστις [persuasion], in *pluralis* he uses πίστεις.[3]—
*JP* IV 4107 (*Pap.* VI A 1) *n.d.*, 1844–45

A new science must be introduced: the Christian art of
speaking,[4] to be constructed *ad modum* [in the manner of] Aristotle's *Rhetoric*. Dogmatics as a whole is a misunderstanding,
especially as it now has been developed.
*In margin: N.B.*
                          —*JP* I 627 (*Pap.* VI A 17) *n.d.*, 1845

*Addition to Pap.* VI A 17:

Reference could be made here also to Carneades' doctrine of
probability. See Ritter, *Geschichte der Philosophie*,[5] III, pp. 677,
678, 679.—*Pap.* VI A 18 *n.d.*, 1845

*In margin of Pap.* VI A 17:

Aristotle places the art of speaking and the media for awakening faith (πίστις) in relation to probability so that it is concerned (in contrast to knowledge) with what can happen in a
different way. Christian eloquence will be distinguished from
the Greek in that it is concerned only with *improbability*, with
showing that it is improbable, in order that one can then *believe*

it. Here probability is to be rejected just as much as improbability in the other, but both have in common the distinction from knowledge.[6]—*JP* I 628 (*Pap.* VI A 19) *n.d.*, 1845


### Conclusion—Enthymeme—Decision

### A Trilogy

This will be an investigation of importance for my theory of the leap and of the difference between a dialectical transition and a transition of pathos.

In the final analysis, what I call a transition of pathos Aristotle[7] called an enthymeme. Perhaps. How remarkable, since I am now reading about enthymeme for the first time in Aristotle's *Rhetoric.*—*JP* III 2353 (*Pap.* VI A 33) *n.d.*, 1845


See journal, p. 158 n., p. 130 [*Pap.* VI A 1; V A 47].

VI
A 147
60

1. A little about the contradictions in the upbuilding address. The relationship to scholarship—which categories may be used.

Here a little about my upbuilding discourses, that they were not sermons. (Objections have been made to this without bearing in mind that for this reason the title was not put that way—but upbuilding discourses.)

It is of equal merit to be a good speaker and a good listener:

in scholarship as many results as possible, in religious address as few results as possible, just as strong in the immediate as the reflective, and one must above all have existed [*existeret*] in both.

The one is a work of art; the other a work of scholarship.
Situation: that Hegel in punishment for his attack upon the religious would have to deliver an upbuilding discourse.

VI
A 147
61

—*JP* I 630 (*Pap.* VI A 147) *n.d.*, 1845

*Report*

This[8] was laid aside for the present. Would get to be too discursive to serve as a kind of introduction to my few discourses. Must be worked out separately and deal essentially with religious address.—*JP* V 5785 (*Pap.* VI B 132) *n.d.*, 1845

*From sketch:*

Remembrance of the God-fearing is a benediction.[9]—*Pap.* VI B 147 *n.d.*, 1844–45

*From sketch:*

VI
B 148
233
VI
B 148
234

Funeral address for a girl who remained faithful to the beloved, although he, far away in the East Indies, at first kept up a correspondence with her for two years and later married someone else. The whole thing had been a secret between him and her. She was some thirty years old, and it was a falling in love in early youth.

A Miss Nielsen (Giødwad[10] has spoken of her.) Governor Hansen[11] (?) was the man

a passage in Shakespeare that tells of a young girl whose whole life was a blank page, but the worm gnawed. The place is marked in my copy.[12]

—*Pap.* VI B 148 *n.d.*, 1844–45

*From sketch:*

Funeral address for the king's deceased valet

to be humorously constructed. —The royal dignity. He was His Majesty's faithful servant (in the same sense as that is also said of a prime minister).

—*Pap.* VI B 149 *n.d.*, 1844–45

*From sketch:*

*Come here, all you who* **labor** *and are* **burdened**[13] (a burdened conscience).—*Pap*. VI B 151 *n.d.*, 1844–45

*From sketch:*

*"That we might learn to sorrow over our sins"*

The prayer in the chancel doorway.
—*Pap*. VI B 152 *n.d.*, 1844–45

*From sketch:*

Funeral address for Anna the prophetess, Phanuel's daughter[14]

—*Pap*. VI B 153 *n.d.*, 1844–45

*From sketch:*

And we are all much too worried about what we will eat.[15] The son of poverty says hungrily: What will we eat, and the satiated son of wealth says: What will I eat tomorrow?—*Pap*. VI B 155 *n.d.*, 1844–45

*From sketch:*

### Confessional Discourse

. . . . . When someone starts out on a long journey, we wish him good fortune*—but the few steps up to the altar: What, indeed, could happen in so doing? And yet it is the most dangerous journey. That he did not find the forgiveness of sin! That he could not forgive himself for it!

*so much, after all, can happen in the long time

—*Pap*. VI B 162 *n.d.*, 1844–45

*From sketch:*

VI
B 163
239
. . . . . But this is what is lacking—no one *wonders* anymore. They journey to far countries and tell us about it, and we make comparisons and marvel over the dissimilarity. Is this to wonder over *God?* When a man lived in some isolated place and saw only one single tree, one little shrub, perhaps a running brook, how could he not marvel—over God. The smaller the object that prompts one to marvel over God, the more one marvels over God.

VI
B 163
240

When that favorite of fortune, who rose from poverty and insignificance on a little island to become emperor of the most powerful countries, when he led the troops and, in order to inspire them, said: Four hundred generations are looking down upon you[16]—ah, just to repeat it makes one shudder—how it must have inflamed the fighters! But when we say to someone: God in heaven looks down and sees what you are doing—no one marvels, no one is moved, it is as if it meant nothing—and yet does not the eternal mean more than 4,000 years?

The forgiveness of sins is proclaimed—forgiveness—but who marvels at it? No one. No one says: Is it possible—oh, is it really possible? No one believes and says: It is impossible, it is impossible!

No one wonders; no one is offended.—*JP* II 1341 (*Pap.* VI B 163) *n.d.*, 1844–45

*From sketch:*

God is the one who raises up and the one who casts down.

*The one raised up before God—and the one cast down.*
                            —*Pap.* VI B 165 *n.d.*, 1844–45

*From sketch:*

### Confessional Discourses

Peter's denial.[17]

To deny oneself is regarded as a triviality (not like thievery, murder, whoring, etc.), and yet it is a dreadful guilt and is actually to lose one's ideality and become a nonsensical something.

—Pap. VI B 166 n.d., 1844–45

*From sketch:*

3 Discourses on the text of the Canaanite woman[18]

No. 1
He said not even one word.

No. 2
The disciples said: Send her away.

No. 3
Be it done unto you as you wished.

—Pap. VI B 167 n.d., 1844–45

*From sketch:*

No. 1
The denial at the first crowing of the cock.

No. 2
The denial at the second crowing of the cock.

No. 3
The denial at the third crowing of the cock.[19]

—Pap. VI B 168 n.d., 1844–45

*From sketch:*

Confessional Discourse

On the **comfort** in suffering as guilty.

Socrates' words to Xanthippe: Would you prefer that I should be guilty.[20]

The two robbers on the cross: We are receiving what we have deserved [*forskyldt*]; he is suffering as guilty [*skyldig*].[21]

—*Pap.* VI B 169 *n.d.*, 1844–45

*From sketch:*

We suffer for our sins, but this one suffers as innocent.

These words are not said by some sage, by a famous thinker etc.
  it is, as everyone knows, a dialogue between two robbers.

Whether it is hardest to suffer as guilty or to suffer as innocent?

—*Pap.* VI B 170 *n.d.*, 1844–45

*From sketch:*

the words from Joel: Return to the Lord with all your heart, with fasting, weeping, and mourning.[22]
(For the confessional discourse)
To fast, that is, to die to multiplicity, to the judgment of plurality etc.

—*Pap.* VI B 171 *n.d.*, 1844–45

*From sketch:*

### Confession

Confess the sins to one another.

—*Pap.* VI B 172 *n.d.*, 1844–45

*From sketch:*

The fire of repentance and the accusing conscience is like that Grecian fire[23] that could not be put out with water—so, too, this one can be extinguished only with tears.—*JP* III 3785 (*Pap.* VI B 173) *n.d.*, 1844–45

*From sketch:*

The best divine worship is to think lowly of oneself and highly of God: as a sinner—the Holy One.—*Pap.* VI B 174 *n.d.*, 1844–45

*From sketch:*

*To concern* **oneself about** *oneself.*[24]
                    —*JP* IV 4425 (*Pap.* VI B 175) *n.d.*, 1844–45

*From sketch:*

This generation is like children in the marketplace; they will not mourn—will not dance.[25]—*Pap.* VI B 176 *n.d.*, 1844–45

*From sketch:*

One undertakes to judge the teacher instead of concerning oneself about oneself and the meaning of the teaching for oneself.—*Pap.* VI B 177 *n.d.*, 1844–45

*Faith's saving secret*

On the Gospel about the hemorrhaging woman
     she *said softly to herself:* If I only touch[26]

The rest of us *recite loudly a whole creed of faith* and perhaps say *quite softly to ourselves: What can it help.*—*Pap.* VI B 181 *n.d.*, 1844–45

Preface[27] by Johannes de Silentio.[28]

> This preface is a flyleaf title, which is not to be bound into the volume
> —to write it is an unpleasant task that I do only out of long-standing friendship for the Magister.

In many respects our age lives in a great multiplicity of categories, some pagan, some Christian, some nonsensical (es-

VI
B 128
217

VI
B 128
218

pecially with regard to marriage). Religious discourse contains a multiplicity of contradictions undetected by the pastor.

In actual occasional discourses some things cannot very well be said because of the presence of the specific persons before one. Therefore the reverse is done here: the stated individualities are created by the discourse. Nor would any harm be done if a marriage ceremony was sometimes of such a nature that it prevented another person from going ahead and getting married.

Magister K. has not had opportunity to practice what the preachers understand by occasional discourses (they do not grasp the occasion but rummage around with names and dates and titles: the honorable bridegroom)—when one sees what the pastors make of the occasion richly offered them, one is tempted sometimes to risk an attempt.

If anyone has any objection, perhaps he will address himself to me, the undersigned, Joh. d. S., and leave the Magister out of it, and also his discourses, which he in every way seeks to keep from becoming the object of discussion and especially of reviews.—*Pap.* VI B 128 *n.d.*, 1845

VI B 129 218 *Malpractices* in the Oratorical Address

> It is said that Paul is one of the most *remarkable* of the apostles, which means that there are esthetic categories together with the dogmatic categories.

One admires an expression such as the figure of a race at the racetrack.[29] Even if one does not admire it as foolishly as Münter[30] did the other day, the esthetic is a mistake. —The apostolic quality is authority—not brilliance, because I, too, can
VI B 129 219 toss off just as striking a figure, to say nothing of the Greeks.
God knows what one would really think if someone begins to admire the matchlessness of such an expression.—*JP* I 635 (*Pap.* VI B 129) *n.d.*, 1845

*Addition to Pap.* VI B 129:

That one makes the movement of infinite reflection and then suddenly ends up with categories that speak of the endearing goodness that does not know how good it is itself, the purity that is ignorant of sin. (The first of which is within the category of immediacy; the second is pure nonsense.)—*JP* V 5783 (*Pap.* VI B 130) *n.d.*, 1845

Divisions[31]

(1) Subject of the Address
(2) The Listener
(3) The Speaker

—*JP* V 5784 (*Pap.* VI B 131) *n.d.*, 1845

*From draft:*

*Something about Spiritual Occasional
Discourses* [Crossed out with pencil: *Eloquence*]
by
Johannes de Silentio[*]

VI
B 133
219

What I intend to say here perhaps could best be regarded as a foreword to a book, and regarded as such I in turn prefer it to be regarded as a flyleaf title page, which is not to be bound into the volume when the book is bound. The decision to write it is of course my own; otherwise I could leave it alone. But the person who has prompted me to make it is Magister S. Kierkegaard, who expressly has requested it of me. That is, he himself intends to try his hand at a few such discourses, and his wish was that this step would need no introduction whatever. Yet by omitting it he fears to see his attempt dragged into the context of reviewing by a possible critic; and by attaching the introduction to the undertaking itself he fears that this undertaking in all its insignificance would acquire a wrong significance through this introduction, which, as it were, would invite the review, which could possibly have the effect that the

VI
B 133
220

[*] *Penciled in margin*: with continual reference to Aristotle's *Rhetoric*.

little book would have far too many readers and above all not a
single uncritical reader. But this would be a sad mistake. Just as
it is required of the good speaker that he himself be his own
severest critic, so it is required of the good listener or reader,
even if he were the sharpest intellect, that he renounce reviews.
In relation to the religious, it is perhaps not so much a matter of
the choice of pastor or the choice of book or of being led or not
allowing oneself to be disturbed during this deliberation, as it is
a matter of this choice: to will to allow oneself to be built up.
Therefore, without wanting the following comments to de-
clare indulgence for the speaker, I am convinced that the person
who will allow himself to be built up, even if he heard a perhaps
mediocre pastor or read a perhaps mediocre devotional book,
will be built up. The danger is that someone may be disturbed
in this regard or in remaining, resolute, in his choice. Therefore,
together with the Magister, I consider being a good listener
just as great as being a good speaker,[32] and perhaps at times the
former is even the greater, that is, if it is ordinarily more difficult to receive a good and beneficial and upbuilding impression
from something unsound than to keep oneself in oneself,* even
if one encountered misunderstanding on every side. What all
this means is more or less this: I will act as a buffer [*tage stødet
af*]. It is my wish that no one will be hurt [*støde sig*] and that
there might be no offense [*Anstød*]; but if anyone has anything
negative to say, my request is that he will address himself to me
and above all not bring the discourses themselves into association with our differences, no more than I shall appeal to or refer
to them. If the critic should think that more concrete examples
are necessary to illustrate the discussion, I am sure that he will
be so kind as to sketch them himself, which he can very easily
do. I for my part shall reciprocate to the best of my ability,
because I do not write discourses, and sketches indeed have no
other aim or, even more definitely, they have precisely the aim
of wanting to aid in the discussion.

My name is de Silentio. Thus it is my wish, as it is the
Magister's, that the discourses might themselves find a single

VI
B 133
221

* *In margin:* collected in oneself

reader, that single individual whom they seek, but no comment, which they assuredly are not seeking. And now a direct word. I do not think that anyone dares claim that the Magister is foisting his pamphlets on his contemporaries. I know that he, without consoling himself with the thought of posterity,[33] without the authority to make great demands on his contemporaries, would rather make them upon himself. As for recognition, which it is human to desire and inhuman to reject, I know that he thinks that he has already achieved the highest. His upbuilding discourses, which were not reviewed in any paper or in any way made the subject of comment, were not unfavorably mentioned by the very reverend firm of Kts,[34] which, with regard to recognition, was the highest he had wished and more than he had expected. Although it is now an event in the *past* and time has gone by, he only wishes to stop with that, and with regard to memory he is not so dissatisfied as to forget that it was the only thing he had wished and more than he had expected, and with regard to expectation is not ingeniously engaged in awaiting new heroes, and with regard to himself is convinced that his achievements are far away from the regions where that not unequally revered firm also stands strong, where Prof. Madvig[35] exercises judicial power with authority. Undisturbed by excessive expectations,* he finds it quite in order that he is rarely read** but is appreciative in acknowledgment of the conduct of those who, although readers, yet by silence show true sympathy for a sincere wish. —This wish of his is unchanged.

VI
B 133
222

In the history of warfare, it is supposed to have happened not infrequently that, although the inhabitants of the besieged city were aware of all the enemy's operations and were ready at every moment to defend at every point, there nevertheless was a secret path the defenders had not thought of until they heard the enemies' cry, and the courageous were seized by a panic

---

* *In margin:* unharassed by meaningless life-views that encourage everyone to want to help people by the thousands

** *In margin:* by no means thinks that anyone is harmed by leaving it alone

terror that affects one like a natural force and makes one person stronger than thousands who individually are just as strong as the one person. If our present age is called a struggling age,[36] as it is in fact commonly called, one will, as I do, leave it undecided whether its struggling is for conquest or defense or only rebelliousness—if there actually were such a secret path, it would always be good to be aware of it. I say *if*, because far be it from me to prophesy and warn in addition to raising a hue and cry. It is quite possible that the whole thing is a whim that I have had and belongs nowhere.

The multitudinous political, philanthropic, social, artistic, belletristic, theatrical, Italian-Danish and Danish-Italian, Scandinavian, etc. controversies taking place in our day I leave entirely without comment. But in *scholarship*, and especially *theological scholarship*, one finds that continued quarreling is certainly going on, whether it is speculation that seeks to take possession of the substance of theology, be it by force or by insinuation, or it is theology that seeks to evade an impertinent intimacy plus drinking *Dus* with the executioner.[37] To all appearances no decisive blow is being delivered there. But it still more or less captures the attention of many, and the most outstanding among the devotees of theology enters into this controversy because he thinks that his powers are necessary here, and that the highly placed, who watch over the whole thing, discover with joy some outstanding person in order to place him here because here is the danger.

VI
B 133
223

I am assuming now that it actually is the more competent and outstanding who as teachers* at a university or in some other way dispute on these points in a purely scholarly way—in that case the rest of us are of course secure. The young student will not go astray, because the outstanding ones uphold the good cause and teach the young what is true.

The average young student, of course, cannot be deemed as highly gifted as those outstanding ones, but therefore the apprentices' life-task in the more modest position as a** clergy-

* *In margin:* of theology
** *In margin:* subordinate

man will also be much easier to carry out. *Posito*, I assume, that the irregularity was located here, while the struggling age, persevering and alert in the scholarly battle, safely hands over the easier tasks (*posito* that they were the more difficult) to the less gifted.

From the subordinate servants* of the church we do not feel able to require as much scholarly education as from the assistant professors at the university, and this is quite as it should be. But when that makes us forget what really is required of the teachers of the Church, then confusion is created. In other words, because as much scholarly education is not required, then, besides the more modest education as a scholar, something else could certainly be required that would make the requirement for the pastor just as great as for the professor and would not continue to evaluate him according to his relation to the university because his education as a student is owed to this honorable institution. If scholarliness is overrated, then not only theological students but also the clergy are ranked according to a possible relation to the maximum of being able to become or to be a professor of theology. Woe to the student who does not learn to have lofty ideas about scholarship! Woe to the older person, however often he was disappointed in his trust in those he youthfully venerated as heroes, if he nevertheless does not again cling firmly to his first love and to his first scholarly enthusiasm. But is it right to conclude that the person who admittedly was not altogether capable of being a professor but yet was close to it, is it right to conclude that he *eo ipso* [precisely thereby] was an outstanding servant of the Church?

But scholarship in our day seems to have snatched so much power for itself that even the clergyman who feels the difficulty of his task does not dare divulge it lest what he says be punished by his being looked at pityingly as someone who must repeat his studies with the professor, just like an old person who must

VI
B 133
224

* *In margin:* (namely, the pastors, because I am not at this point thinking of sextons etc., and between pastor and pastor there really ought to be only a relative difference)

go to confirmation classes with the pastor again.[38] Indeed, scholarship presumably wants to snatch so much power for itself that ultimately the clergyman, instead of valuing his task even if a contemporary age does not know how to value it, chooses a frivolous association with scholarship, chooses to rescue himself from his clerical position as a professor *extraordinarius* [without tenure] at an imaginary university, chooses to woo from a pulpit the favor and gratifying applause of a scholarly half-educated public. And if any clergyman crudely chose to preach an anathema upon scholarship, this of course would in turn show that scholarliness had snatched power for itself.

Therefore one sees *the scholarly danger*, but there where the not-so-rigorously developed and less gifted person is to invest his learning, is to make it applicable, is to make what is lofty pronounceable, is to give a definite answer to a simple question, is to take a definite position, there where he heard from the Herr Professor that even scholarship is wobbling, without daring to secure his position by a little scholarly disdaining of someone, as if he were not sufficiently learned, all of which is not deemed to be the easiest of tasks—there is no danger. And because I say *posito*, it of course does not follow that the danger is there; it would not even follow if I said: "It is there."

VI
B 133
225

Let us in the meantime make an imaginary construction [*Experiment*]. I imagine, then, a moderately competent theological professor, whose lectures in the scholarly sense are worthy of honor. Now we shall make the imaginary construction and tell him: Deliver an upbuilding discourse. In order not to bring others into a collective disgrace by jointly venturing a rash statement, I will prefer to take the responsibility upon myself—he cannot do it. It is not even impossible that the Herr Professor will himself admit it and that then everyone, every listening clergyman and every deferential layman, will humble himself under the following superior remark: "I am able to do it, all right; that is not the reason, but the congregation is unable to follow me." That I can well believe, and it is precisely why I conclude: Therefore he cannot do it. Socrates, for example, was not great because he could talk so that no one at all could understand him, nor because he could talk so that the Sophists understood him, but because he could talk with everyone so that everyone understood him, and talk in such a way, please note, that he continually said the same thing. *Unter uns gesagt* [Just between us], Socrates was not a Per Degn, who had fine sand and coarse sand[39]—he did not use much sand at all.

So, then, the reason the Herr Prof. gave appears to me (I speak only in my own name and will not involve anyone in the predicament) to be conceited talk, well suited to nurturing the flesh.[40] It is quite true that the professor will be proud of his scholarship and that he will say of it: I do not wish to make a fool of myself or of it, as if one could in a half hour impart to everyone what costs me, with my superior capacities, time and energy year in and year out, and this is why I hold in contempt any dabbling in what is popular. It is quite right, and it is perhaps to be desired that scholars sometimes want to employ this language in earnest, but if the professor is not prey to an illusion he will add: There are, however, other tasks, such as delivering an upbuilding discourse, a sermon, something I feel the need to hear as well as the simplest person does, and I do not have the gifts and am not trained for that, but I certainly do realize that it can, in altogether the same way, take an exceptionally gifted man's total time and energy just as scholarship takes mine.

In order, however, to make the matter more clear, we can change the imaginary construction a little. Thus, it is not to peasants or the common man the professor is to speak, nor to the half-educated who learnedly prick up their ears in God's house; it is not even to advanced students. It is to *provectiores* [initiates], a select . . . . . —*Pap.* VI B 133 *n.d.*, 1845

*Addition to Pap.* VI B 133:

In order to eliminate any misunderstanding, I can of course change the task a little. It is, then, not to peasants or the common man he is to speak—the imaginary construction is compliant—but neither is it to the half-educated and the cultured who learnedly prick up their ears; it is not even to advanced students. It is to *provectiores* [initiates], a select circle of people, all of whom stand at the pinnacle of scholarship, are

VI
B 133
226

VI
B 137
227

engaged in it every day, and thus are supposed to know a little *en passant* [in passing]. But the task is unchanged: it is no lecture; it is a sermon, an upbuilding discourse. I must urgently beg everyone to be completely convinced that it is not envy, because I cannot be in the audience, that leads me to repeat my answer: he cannot do it. If the reason were anything else than that he lacks the voice, the gestures, the ability to memorize, declamation in the delivery, then, good heavens, the imaginary construction is in every way at his disposition; he is welcome to read it aloud as nasally as he wishes, with wild lectern-gestures; he may even just write it, have it printed—he cannot do it. Strangely enough.

VI
B 137
228

Why can a man who worthily fills his post as professor of theology, why can he not, if he is not a rare exception, deliver a religious discourse if one cancels out eloquence and gives him a scholarly audience—because the transition from scholarship to the upbuilding is not a direct transition, the dissimilarity does not consist of omitting certain technical terms and writing shorter sentences, but the difference is at a place that is never discussed (the requirement of eloquence and accommodation to the listeners is, however, sometimes mentioned), in this, that the categories are completely . . . . . —*Pap.* VI B 137 *n.d.*, 1845

*From sketch:*

6 Discourses
on Imagined Occasions
[*Deleted:* 3 Occasional Discourses on Imagined Occasions]
by
S. Kierkegaard
—*Pap.* VI B 138 *n.d.*, 1844–45

*From draft; see title page:*

Six Discourses on Imagined Occasions
by
S. Kierkegaard
—*JP* V 5778 (*Pap.* VI B 100) *n.d.*, 1845

*From final copy; see title page:*

. . . . . 3 [*changed from:* Six]
                              —*Pap.* VI B 125:1 *n.d.*, 1845

*From margin of final copy; see title page:*

N.B. *Deleted:* To be printed in the same format and in the
     same type as Christian Winther's *Sagn og Sang.*[41]
                              —*Pap.* VI B 125:2 *n.d.*, 1845

*From sketch; see 5:1–25:*

### Preface

VI
B 140
231

Although these discourses (the title of which already discloses
adequately their superfluity, because occasional discourses
where there is no occasion, a fictitious marriage of two who do
not exist at all, a funeral address for a man who has never lived,
a confessional discourse when no one confesses, adequately
disclose how superfluous they are).

VI
B 140
232

    unsolicited, unjustified, unintended, yet it is not without
hope and above all not without bold confidence even though
it does not know the hour when the reader as bridegroom
will visit it.
                              —*Pap.* VI B 140 *n.d.*, 1844–45

*Addition to Pap.* VI B 140:

A woman who embroiders an altar cloth[42]
     does not look at the pearl-stitch embroidery,
     but makes it nevertheless.
                              —*Pap.* VI B 141 *n.d.*, 1844–45

*From sketch; see 5:4–6:*

An occasion makes speakers, and an occasion makes readers,
whereas here the speaker himself must think the occasion and
the reader make it.—*Pap.* VI B 142 *n.d.*, 1844–45

*From sketch; see 5:1–25:*

VI
B 159
237

*Preface*

Although this little book ( . . . . . )

The diligence I expend on the presentation is like that of a woman who embroiders an altar cloth as beautifully as possi- ble; she does not think that anyone in the solemn moment

VI
B 159
238

would look at the sewing, but she does it for her own sake because it is an altar cloth, which she wants to make as beautiful as possible.[43]—*Pap.* VI B 159 *n.d.,* 1844–45

*See 5:1–25:*

*From a Possible Preface to My Occasional Discourses*

. . . . . I wonder if a woman who embroiders a cloth for sacred use does not make every stitch as carefully as possible and perhaps begin over again many times. Yet I wonder if it would not distress her if someone viewed it in the wrong way and looked at the pearl-stitch embroidery instead of at the altar cloth, or saw a defect instead of the altar cloth? She found her priceless joy in doing everything as carefully as possible simply because this work has no meaning and ought to have none; the needlewoman is unable to stitch the meaning into the cloth— the meaning lies within the beholder.[44]—*JP* I 811 (*Pap.* VI A 25) *n.d.,* 1845

*From draft; see 5:1–25:*

VI
B 101
197

*Preface*

Although this little book (occasional discourses, as it has been called, notwithstanding that it does not have the occasion that makes the speaker or the occasion that makes the reader) is[a]

entirely unsolicited and thus in its deficiency entirely unjustified, yet it is not without hope and above all not without
bold confidence. It seeks that single individual whom I with
joy and gratitude call *my* reader, or it does not even seek him.
Unaware of the time and the hour, it waits for that right reader
to come like the bridegroom and to bring the occasion along
with him. Let each do a share.[b] (The time and effort[c] used are
not with the intention of pleasing.) I wonder if a woman who
embroiders a cloth for sacred use does not make every stitch as
carefully as possible and perhaps begin over again many
times.[d] Yet I wonder if it would not distress her if someone
viewed it in the wrong way and looked at the pearl-stitch
embroidery instead of at the altar cloth,[e] and I wonder if she
does not find joy in doing everything so carefully because this
has or ought to have no meaning at all. The meaning lies in the
appropriation,[f] and therefore the book gladly gives of itself;
here there are no[g] mine and thine that separate,[h] [i]because the
appropriation is an even greater, is the triumphant, *giving of
oneself.*

[a]*In margin:* entirely without the support of the circumstances and thus is without assistance in the full development of
the presentation,
    deserted by every circumstance that could assist in the full
development of the presentation
    in its more extensive development
    [b]the reader therefore [*changed from:* perhaps] more.
    [c]are a nothing
    [d]The needlewoman is unable to stitch the meaning into the
cloth; the needlewoman cannot in the least way produce the
effect that it actually is seen as a cloth for sacred use—this lies in
the beholder.
    [e]or saw a defect instead of looking at the altar cloth, al-
though she still found joy in doing everything as carefully as
possible because this has or ought to have no meaning at all.
    [f]hence the book's joyous *giving of itself.*
    [g]worldly
    [h]and prohibit appropriating what is the neighbor's,
                                      —*Pap.* VI B 101 *n.d.*, 1845

VI
B 101
198

*Addition to Pap.* VI B 101:

. . . . . [i]because admiration is in part envy and thus a misunderstanding; and criticism, for all its justification, is really opposition and thus a misunderstanding, but appropriation . . . . .
—*Pap.* VI B 102 *n.d.*, 1845

*Addition to Pap.* VI B 101:

And recognition in a mirror is only a new acquaintance, but not to forget it, something the mirror is incapable of effecting, that is the appropriation—*Pap.* VI B 103 *n.d.*, 1845

*From sketch: see 7, 15:26–29, 29:1–20, 41, 69:*

Discourse at a Confession
at a Wedding
at a Graveside

At a Confession

No. 1. What it means to seek God, when we consider that without purity no human being can see God,[45] and without being a sinner no human being can catch sight of him.

No. 2. To cast all our sorrow upon God and consider [*deleted:* that this is the condition] that we thereby win godly grief.[46]

—*Pap.* VI B 139 *n.d.*, 1844–45

*From sketch:*

No. 1

Confessional Discourse

Cast all your sorrow upon God.

One wishes happiness, good fortune, to a person who is setting out on a long journey—here there are only a few steps from this place of prayer to the altar; what, indeed, could happen there?

We wish that no one, although his sins have been forgiven him, will retain his sins.

—*Pap.* VI B 143 *n.d.*, 1844–45

*From sketch*

. . . . . Truly, O God, you will say to many a one who has done great deeds in your name: I do not know you—but I do not appeal to such things but to what I experienced in the quiet solitude when nothing distracted, when the best in me sought you—will you also say: It is not you, that you do not know me? Do you not remember the time[47]

(to be completed)

was it not you who took it from me—and I sought you in tears.

VI
B 161
238

VI
B 161
239

I seek and desire nothing in the world; I have renounced it to have fellowship with you. Were you to say to me now: I do not know you, then all is lost.

If I had the choice between being the greatest of human beings without you and being a hair that you count (and truly, before you, I am no more than that and do not wish for new disarrangement in order to be more than any other human being), I would choose the latter. Even though I am only so very little to you, to me this little is infinitely much as well as being nothing at all to you, but everything otherwise is nothing to me, absolutely nothing.—*JP* III 3401 (*Pap.* VI B 161) *n.d.*, 1844–45

*From sketch; see 9:1–27:*

## On the Occasion of a Confession

VI
B 164
240

Father in heaven, we turn our minds and our thoughts to you, because it is you who raise up, and it is you who cast down.

Even though we were honored in the world and highly trusted among people, what would all such glory be compared to the unblessedness if you, O righteous God, were not pleased with our own effort, our achievement, our longing, our hope in the world. If we were weighed down, demolished, unappreciated, abandoned, alone with our care in the world, and yet your eye, which sees in secret, rested approvingly on our effort, our achievement, our longing, our hope in the world—what would these adversities be compared to such blessedness! And if we were humiliated and crushed by the thought of our own guilt, if our sins had alienated us from people so that no word of consolation came to our ears, and yet our repentance found the way to your throne, O merciful God, and found grace in your sight—what would these sufferings be compared to such blessedness. Yes, Lord, we turn our minds and our thoughts to you, because it is you who raise up and it is you who cast down, to you Lord, Father, our Father, you who are in heaven.—*JP* III 3402 (*Pap.* VI B 164) *n.d.*, 1844–45

VI<br>B 164<br>241

*From draft; see 9:1–15:30:*

VI<br>B 150<br>234

## Prayer

Father in heaven
How well we know that seeking always has its promise; how much the more, then, seeking you, the one and only giver and guarantor of all the promises. How well we know that the seeker is not always to go out into the world, since the more holy that is which he seeks, the closer it is to him, and if he seeks you, O God, you are closest of all to him. But we know also that seeking always has its terror; how much the more, then, seeking you, you Mighty One. If even the person who in thought puts his trust in his kinship with you, if even he does not without quaking venture out into those decisions when he seeks your footprint in the powers of existence; if even he whom you called your friend because he walked in your sight, if even he does not without trembling seek friendship's reunion with you, you Lord of Heaven; if even the one praying, who

VI<br>B 150<br>235

loves you with his whole heart, does not without anxiety venture into prayer's struggle with you, you Mighty One; if even the one dying, for whom you yourself exchange life, still does not without shuddering relinquish the temporal when he seeks you, you Terrifying One; if even the wretched one whom the world gave only suffering* does not without terror take refuge in God—how, then, does the sinner dare to seek you, you Righteous One. But that is why he does not seek you in those ways but seeks you in the confession of sins. Here is the place, how still.

(No one can see God without purity, and yet no one can catch sight of him without confessing his sin.)

*with sheer wretchedness behind him.

—*JP* III 3398 (*Pap.* VI B 150) *n.d.*, 1844–45

*From sketch:*

Motif

My listener. Imagine that you yourself are going to deliver a discourse to another person—this can also become a discourse.

Now you and I begin. So you would first say: Test yourself, and then you would help him a little with your experiences.

—*Pap.* VI B 180 *n.d.*, 1844–45

*Deleted from margin in final copy; see 11:6:*

. . . . . in a distracted mind's or an evil conscience's pact with the multiplicity or with evil . . . . .

—*Pap.* VI B 125:5 *n.d.*, 1845

*From sketch; see 11:25:*

Mynster[48] preached yesterday, February 9, 1845, on this text: We have nothing but possess everything.[49] Excellent, but he did not make the move that could have become very useful, especially as an introduction: Perhaps there was someone who

possessed everything and yet had nothing.[50]—*Pap.* VI B
157 February 10, 1845

*From draft; see 12:3–15:27:*

Thus the confessor seeks God in the confession of sins, and
the confession is the road and is a biding place on the road of
salvation, where one pauses and collects one's thoughts. In
connection[*] with this and as preparation for it, we shall talk
about

*What it means to seek God* and define it more precisely . . . . .
[*]*Penciled in margin:* N.B.
                                    —*Pap.* VI B 104:1 *n.d.,* 1845

*From draft; see 13:18–27:*

It is as a pagan has said, a pagan whose name is inseparable
from the idea of conquests and power, when his opponent
died: There he robbed me of the[*] most glorious victory I ever
would have won, that I could forgive him.[**]

[*]*In margin:* Caesar said this about Cato when the latter committed suicide.

*In margin:* [**]And as someone else has said: Because I love
[*deleted:* this person so] much [*deleted:* that I grant him the
highest power one person can have over another], I will not ask
for forgiveness. My wrong perhaps was not so great, forgiveness perhaps not so difficult to obtain, but if it is not obtained,
then the wrong is infinite, the forgiveness an infinite
predominance—*Pap.* VI B 106:2 *n.d.,* 1845

*From draft; see 20:6–16:*

. . . . . sought.*
*a little rhetoric as in the part about wishing; the structure is
suitable to that part.

*In margin:* Everyone once in his youth had this recklessness in
venturing, and is the person wiser who ventures nothing.—
*Pap.* VI B 104:3 *n.d.,* 1845

*From draft; see 21:3–22:*

In books and book jargon it may of course be said that it is a bygone formation and thus one is finished—at least with the book, but in life it is not this way.*

*In margin:* *Everyone has experienced it at some time when youth departed—was the person better who did not come this far—rhetoric *ad modum* [in the manner of] the two previous passages.

At youth's turn of the year . . . . .

—*Pap.* VI B 104:4 *n.d.*, 1845

*Continuation of Pap.* VI B 104:4; *see 22:30–23:8:*

So the wonder is gone—but you, my listener, you of course know that we have just now come to the true wonder—that is, that you are there.

*In margin:* I cannot deceive you if you have [not] forgotten the preceding.

it is not claptrap and the discourse quietly . . . . .

—*Pap.* VI B 105 *n.d.*, 1845

VI
B 105
199

VI
B 105
200

*From draft; see 25:9–21:*

. . . . . looks down at him or rather sees through him and makes a judgment about him. And this wonder and this fear that expand and compress you, you alone in the whole world, because you have become alone with the Omnipresent One, this wonder the discourse cannot teach you.—*Pap.* VI B 108:2 *n.d.*, 1845

*From draft; see 26:35–38:*

*Penciled in margin:* Something like this has certainly been experienced at some time by everyone who was liquidated in bankruptcy and from whom the utmost was required and at every point—alas, and even if many do not think they have come to this extremity, did they all became wiser, also those who according to what the earnest one says (Bishop Mynster, Spiellerup, I, p. 3[51]).—*Pap.* VI B 108:3 *n.d.*, 1845

*From draft; see 29:36–30:3:*

The authority who watches over justice sometimes uses spies whom he has in his power, with whom he has a little secret—and likewise the consciousness of sin is sometimes the leash with which God holds his highly trusted ones. But that authority does not care much for the spies themselves but only about their serving him—God does not do this.—*Pap.* VI B 108:4 *n.d.,* 1845

*From draft; see 30:17–22:*

The greatest sinner. People have laughed at the two bald-headed men who disputed about a comb. They have laughed and will laugh if two poor wretches would dispute about who was the more wretched—and now to dispute about who was the greatest sinner. Yes, it is indeed laughable, but it is not laughable that we have managed to get the ludicrous mixed in where it does not belong.—*Pap.* VI B 108:5 *n.d.,* 1845

*From draft; see 32:23:*

. . . . . , but the earnest one observes himself [*deleted:* just as the observations of the earnest one[52] also are[*]]. Thus the matter becomes something different; indeed, everything becomes so changed, as the earnest one has said, "that the issue becomes the justifying of God before the world, not a concern about justifying oneself before God."[**]

[*]*Deleted in margin:* Bishop Mynster.
[**]*In margin:* Bishop Mynster.

                                         —*Pap.* VI B 108:7 *n.d.,* 1845

*From final copy; see 32:25:*

*Changed from:* the earnest one has said it,* . . .
*Note. Bishop Mynster

                                         —*Pap.* VI B 125:7 *n.d.,* 1845

*Deleted from final copy; see 35:31:*

And if anyone notes that darkness falls upon his soul, let him be silent, because in this condition he ought not to speak.—*Pap.* VI B 125:8 *n.d.*, 1845

*In margin of draft; see 37:26:*

A poet has so beautifully said of a girl: Her young soul was tested gold. This is doubtful, because how can the young soul be *tested*. But if she was rare in this way, or if all people were like this, what scant consolation, but this is certain, that whether all were thus or only the rare ones, everyone can become tested gold if he is faithful!—*Pap.* VI B 108:10 *n.d.*, 1845

*From draft; see 37:35:*

*Penciled:* see a quarter-sheet draft [*missing*],
which is to be greatly developed in order
to stimulate
                              —*Pap.* VI B 108:11 *n.d.*, 1845

*Deleted from margin in final copy; see 46:15:*

Marriage, however, concerns everyone, also the one, if there is such, who resolved never to enter into it.—*Pap.* VI B 125:9 *n.d.*, 1845

*From draft; see 48:38–49:20:*

The person[*] who grew old in the faithful [service] of love and, tested in much, conquered and won the incorruptible beauty of faithfulness, about whom one may truly use the noble poet's somewhat sentimental statement in regard to the young girl, that her young soul was tested gold, truly uses the expression that she was tested gold, when such a venerable one, who remained faithful to her husband and her commitment according to the dictates of her own conscience, when she says with the gentle, friendly [*counsel*] of old age: My children, love conquers everything—then she may very well stir the young people and deceive them a little, because when she says it, it seems so easy, but if they take the saying in vain, then experience steps between them and her and says: Step aside here, veneration, and teaches them the difficulty, and points to her and says, "See here, love has conquered everything."

[*]*In margin:* must be a man.

—*Pap.* VI B 112:1  *n.d.*, 1845

*From draft; see 54:1–55:6:*

VI<br>B 112:2<br>203

. . . . . of the insignificance of the common task.* Consider it [a marriage], there where death almost seems to come opportunely, and yet it is not this way. Ah, what a sorrowful situation, to have to admit to oneself that death is not the greatest danger, and then perhaps sense again through death that one still loved what one lost. Consider a marriage in which, instead of an honest exchange, misunderstanding transacts its sorry business and estranges each from the other in suspicion, mistrust, and ungentleness and impatience and distraction, although they perhaps still love each other. And was it always poverty and straitened circumstances that caused this? Ah, a marriage is sometimes maintained in wealth and abundance— to call to mind an old expression about the honeymoon [*Hvedebrødsdagene*, the wheat-bread days]—a marriage that still is in all abundance although on bread and water and helps each of them interdependently to this suffering of punishment. Was it always only sadness over wayward children that finally came to be like a curse between the parents themselves—ah, it is certainly also the case that the rare good fortune of having well-behaved children was of no help to the parents.[**]

VI<br>B 112:2<br>204

*In margin:* *and while the grass grows the mare starves

*Penciled in margin:* N.B. to be developed further in milder terms.

[**]*In margin:* was it only the years.

was it only an original misrelation in age, education, social class,

—*Pap.* VI B 112:2  *n.d.*, 1845

*From sketch; see 56:17–20:*

But perhaps someone will find it insulting to speak to lovers this way, to do it enviously instead of admiring and eulogizing.

One can be justified in this discourse but not justified in discourse generally.—*Pap.* VI B 113:1 *n.d.*, 1845

*From sketch; see 56:27–57:13:*

The love the poets describe is rarely found in its purity in the world.—*Pap.* VI B 113:2 *n.d.*, 1845

*From sketch; see 57:27–30:*

The marriage ceremony proclaims sin
  and instead of talking about death in connection with unhappiness in marriage one should talk about sin.
                              —*Pap.* VI B 113:3 *n.d.*, 1845

*From sketch; see 57:34–38:*

The *rebirth* of love in resolution
                      —*Pap.* VI B 113:4 *n.d.*, 1845

*From sketch; see 58:9–26:*

Perhaps someone will say that the discourse may be really beautiful but the speaker lacks earnestness. Let us bear this in mind, because self-understanding, after all, is also necessary in order to make a resolution, including self-understanding with regard to the many confusing impressions from life.—*Pap.* VI B 113:5 *n.d.*, 1845

*In margin of Pap. VI B 113:5; see 58:9–26:*

You say, my listener, "It takes much earnestness in order for such a discourse to make the right impression"—correct—

namely, in the reader and the listener.—*Pap*. VI B 113:6 *n.d.*,
1845


*From sketch; see 58:34–59:10:*

in childhood—freedom's choice in life.
pure earnestness through the idea
                                   —*Pap*. VI B 113:8 *n.d.*, 1845


*From draft; see 59:11–60:5:*

Now life's confusion begins. The most diverse things are
proclaimed in the world, the most diverse prototypes appear.
If you want to flit about capriciously, then bear in mind that the
human being is no bird, and least of all a married man, and
every human being has to have his abiding place, and without
resolution he never acquires it. But the person who wants to
enter into marriage is, after all, at the age when it is about time
to have a resolution, and if this step cannot help him, alas, then
it perhaps will never come.—*Pap*. VI B 114:1 *n.d.*, 1845


*From draft; see 60:12–19:*

VI
B 114:2
205

VI
B 144:2
206

If it is adversity, one can of course learn defiance from it. If it
is the responsibility of marriage, well, one can learn that best
from a child, but sometimes also a father learns to become a
tyrant just because of the unconditional obedience the child
must show. If it is all the little troubles that are supposed to
educate us, well, they also come accompanied by things that
injure and delay us and waste our time, and we learn sullenness
from them. So also with guidance in life.—*Pap*. VI B
114:2 *n.d.*, 1845


*From draft; see 61:14–32:*

Now the one guiding is perhaps too old, now too young, for
you. If that is what you thought about the one speaking here,
then he is of course guiltless, because he especially wants you to

have no confidence in him. Alas, if you did have it, perhaps much, and now suppose that he still went astray, suppose that he crashed, then his fall would perhaps drag you along if you had had much confidence—see, this is why you must never build upon sand.

*In margin:* One person means so well, but he is weak; another has power, but he does not mean what he says.—*Pap.* VI B 114:3 *n.d.*, 1845

*From draft; see 63:16–67:33:*

People are so eager to admire, and who has not frequently thought of what was the most beautiful and praiseworthy in the world, what one could have joy in admiring and from which one could oneself benefit, what was noble in the beholder's eye and ennobled the beholder himself when he looked at it worthily. It is self-evident that one does not admire good fortune and distinction and renown and glorious gifts and things like that, because they cannot be admired in this way; admiration here is either a foolishness that wastes its own time or an envy that retards itself. And yet everyone wishes an object of admiration, whether a man or a woman, because even this difference is canceled here. And in turn one will not admire youth, because it has its testing time before it, and so one prefers to choose one's object of admiration among the elderly.

My listener, think of an old man. Those who were acquainted with his famous and splendid life from an earlier time told that good fortune had carried him through the world. Some by reason of personal envy became impatient about it and thought that one had it easy then, but yet they did not dare to deny that no one in the country was more worthy of the high positions he held than he was. It is not this we want to admire. But look, now he is an old man, and then it must be said of him that he was not more earnest[53] than he once was in the glorious beginning of this remarkable career. It is not the remarkable person we admire, not his[*] name, but that he, carried along

[*]*In margin:* immortal

VI
B 118
206

VI
B 118
207

by good fortune, learned earnestness. One can learn much from good fortune, also to become something great in the world, but to learn earnestness is truly the most difficult of all. That being bowed down by life at an early age, that an unhappy childhood, that depression, that the sorrows of life, that hard work can help a person to become earnest—indeed, that is more readily explained. But if life removes everything that one is accustomed to regard as an aid to earnestness and gives everything that is most tempting to light-mindedness, to arrogance, to satiety in order to become something great—then to become earnest, yes, that is great. And if you will ask which earnestness is the purest, you will no doubt answer precisely this, because all other earnestness can be slightly dubious, but this earnestness that does not come into existence in a hastening of terror, is not doleful in suffering, is not bowed down and sighing, but came into existence on the day of good fortune—indeed, how is it possible. Yes, it came into existence on the day of good fortune by way of the resolution, and therefore it is the healthiness of an eternal life, and therefore to admire it is beneficial.

And even with regard to marriage, if you were to ask which is the most beautiful, I would mention the venerable married couple whose earnestness in the evening of life must be said to be the same as on the day of good fortune when the resolution came into existence and remained with them unchanged, while good fortune accompanied them without interruption. If we do not agree that to learn earnestness from good fortune is the most admirable, at least you will not confuse the impression by thinking that then it is an easy matter, but if on the contrary you needed suffering, you will perceive that it was an alleviation, but in such a prototype you will also have the proper test of your own earnestness, that it is not gloomy, that it is not envious, that it is not bitter, that it is not a simple copy of life's adversities, because earnestness is never that.

*Deleted:* But married life in the world is so very different; yet there is one resolution common to all, that love [*Kjerlighed*] conquers everything, and this resolution is its beginning and

VI
B 118
208

contains a true conception of life and of itself, and a true conception of God—then the end indeed becomes like the beginning, and love has conquered everything.

—*Pap.* VI B 118 *n.d.*, 1845

*From sketch; see 69:1–77:38:*

## No. 2

### Graveside Discourse

A godly discourse should never be divisive. Poor people who go out to the graveyard and take food along. The beautiful simplicity of this, as if it were also a pleasure trip to the forest.

to unite contradictions

What shall I say out there where everything is eloquence, more powerful than a human being's voice. (Situations, see journal [*Pap.* V A 35, 56 (pp. 109–10)]—the short inscriptions on the graves)

In the grave there is no recollection; who can praise God among the dead—
   (1)  see, this is why he did it while he was living
   (2)  therefore we shall recollect him.

—*Pap.* VI B 144 *n.d.*, 1844–45

*Deleted from sketch; see 73:22–76:35:*

The jest implicit in the thought that when I am, death is not, and when death is, I am not.

as if death could not get hold of one, because suffering and adversity do not speak this way.

*The earnest thought of death*

The earnestness is not to die but to think oneself dying,* since another's dying provides only mood. The concept of earnestness is really illuminated here.

VI
B 120:1
209

### Death's Decision

VI
B 120:1
210
*The young man Jean Paul tells about, who dreamed on New Year's Eve that he was an old man and was improved. The emperor, Karl V, who had himself buried alive.—*Pap.* VI B 120:1 *n.d.*, 1845

*From draft; see 74:3–75:2:*

VI
B 119:1
208
VI
B 119:1
209
No other power is like this. Call death an archer—well, erotic love is also an archer, but it hits surely and gets at the wounded one. Call death a friend—well, a friend does become involved with the other. Call it an enemy, a struggle, a suffering; yet all these things still exist and the sufferer, too, still exists, but death is tricked in this way. Right here, however, is the earnestness, and death's earnestness is different from life's earnestness,[*] because it is not death that is earnest, but the thought of death.

[*]The imperfection of life's earnestness is that one fancies oneself to be earnest.—*Pap.* VI B 119:1 *n.d.*, 1845

*From draft; see 75:35–76:13:*

. . . . . lot. The way death otherwise occupies a person, almost jesting in the most light-minded fancy or bowing in deep sorrow, it occupies him in mood, not in earnestness.—*Pap.* VI B 119:3 *n.d.*, 1845

*From draft; see 77:19–39:*

. . . . . practicing this thought
all comparison is jest.
—*Pap.* VI B 119:4 *n.d.*, 1845

*From sketch; see 76:14–33:*

My listener, a poet has told of a young man who dreamed one night that on a New Year's Eve he contemplated his life as an old man, and lo, it was wasted, and he awoke in terror—well, it was a dream, and he was saved. —An emperor had himself buried before he died—so let it be you yourself, for is it not true that much is said about the dead, which you do not believe, that is always good, and you find it beautiful, but is it therefore true; if the dead one could hear it, would it not shame him.

—*Pap.* VI B 179 *n.d.*, 1844–45

*Deleted from sketch; see 78:19–79:23:*

(1) it is decisive.
one sees that immediately in the personification of death

not like the angel of hope, who beckons, not of joy, who looks around, not of recollection.

—*Pap.* VI B 120:18 *n.d.*, 1845

*Deleted from sketch; see 78:19–80:6:*

(1) Death decisive.
the dead one is not flushed in sleep—he does not stir, not because his clothes fit tightly, as the coffin does.
The expression of mood: *death is a sleep*
*a night* in which no work can be done.
—The expression of earnestness: *all is over*, and no nonsense or wasting of time

—*Pap.* VI B 120:10 *n.d.*, 1845

*From sketch; see 78:25–79:6:*

So, then, all is over; if to one who is living it perhaps often seems that a perfect conclusion is not to be found, death is able to do this.—*Pap.* VI B 145 *n.d.*, 1844–45

*Deleted from sketch: see 78:36–79:4:*

up to here

the meaning is at an end
concluded
stand still
—*Pap.* VI B 120:2 *n.d.*, 1845


*From sketch; see 77:1–6:*

It is difficult to find one saying in which all the countless
generations of living individuals can be united; whereas all the
*dead* are united in *one* saying to the living: *Stand still!*—*Pap.* VI
B 178 *n.d.*, 1844–45


*Deleted from draft; see 79:1–6:*

Although it is difficult to unite into one all the different
sayings of countless millions of people, all the dead have this
one saying, Stand still. Although it is impossible to unite all the
various endeavors of countless people and the various results of
the same in one expression, all the dead say: Now all is over.—
*Pap.* VI B 120:19 *n.d.*, 1845


*Deleted from sketch; see 79:7–9:*

Death is no inexperienced youth whom you could impress
with the importance of your life, dumbfound, etc.—*Pap.* VI B
120:9 *n.d.*, 1845


*Deleted from margin in final copy; see 79:12:*

The mirror of life at times gives back to the vain one his
flattering dissimilarity, but in the mirror of death all look
alike.—*Pap.* VI B 125:10 *n.d.*, 1845

*Deleted from sketch; see 79:12–80:17:*

(1) it is constant.

　has one ever seen it change color, or, moved by something, change countenance, and yet what has it not experienced.

　if it is in the midst of the work, or a little was lacking, or one single word you have wanted to say all your life.
—Pap. VI B 120:3 n.d., 1845

*From draft; see 79:23:*

. . . . . there is no thought of whether its color has become paler or the years have marked its face—no, it is unchanged.
*In margin:* or that it has become thinner
—Pap. VI B 122:1 n.d., 1845

*From final copy; see 82:2:*

. . . . . *the injurious anesthesia* . . . . .
*In margin: epileptic seizure*
—Pap. VI B 125:11 n.d., 1845

*Deleted from sketch; see 83:14–94:17:*

(2) it is indefinable; with reference to what weapon it will use, it is definable in earnest only for the earnest one
—Pap. VI B 120:4 n.d., 1845

*Deleted from sketch; see 85:14–96:17:*

(2) Death indefinable.

[*Deleted:* (a) equal]　enthusiasm and sadness
recognizes no social　—the earnestness that it
position and ages　is oneself

VI<br>B 120:11<br>211

(b) indefinable. Mood: capacious fantasy view
of a nothing [*deleted:* a night].
The expression of earnestness
to live every day as if it were
the last, and the first in a long
life. The substance of the
work.
—*Pap.* VI B 120:11 *n.d.*, 1845


*Deleted from sketch; see 86:17–88:9:*

That death makes us all equal may be comforting for hate,
which seeks this powerless revenge, for the enthusiasm of despair. but is mood, . . . . .
—*Pap.* VI B 120:12 *n.d.*, 1845


*From draft; see 89:14–15:*

. . . . . this shudder is in the life of nature and in the life of
spirit.
*In margin:* horror vacui [abhorrence of a vacuum]
—*Pap.* VI B 122:2 *n.d.*, 1845


*From draft; see 89:18–21:*

. . . . . to be a day laborer among the living and not a king
among the dead.
—*Pap.* VI B 122:3 *n.d.*, 1845


*From draft; see 89:21–90:4:*

*In pencil:* and no comparison has that impelling power.
*In pencil:* The woman's mirror—and the ascetic's death's-
head *In ink:*—alone far away from friendship
and sympathy in the equality of death.
—*Pap.* VI B 122:4 *n.d.*, 1845

*From draft; see 92:21–36:*

. . . . . discovers death in this game of tag, now forgets it again.

                              —*Pap.* VI B 122:5 *n.d.*, 1845

*From draft; see 93:6–11:*

. . . . . and sleeping secure at night. Similarly, it is not earnestness either when the idler becomes addicted to strong drink and in such a drugged condition is, with regard to his spiritual life, basically [like] the person when he weakened his consciousness so it could not endure the earnest impression of the wondrous.—*Pap.* VI B 122:6 *n.d.*, 1845

VI
B 122:6
214

VI
B 122:6
215

*From draft; see 94:11–13:*

. . . . . ., the enigma is solved; indeed, whether he himself is young or old or handsome or ugly or anything like that is not very indeterminable and very difficult to solve.

The finite spirit cannot endure the ordinary view of death; then thought is confused . . . . . —*Pap.* VI B 122:7 *n.d.*, 1845

*Deleted from sketch; see 96:18–97:3:*

(3) it is inexplicable, that is, it provides no explanation
      only the earnest one can in earnest have the explanation
                              —*Pap.* VI B 120:5 *n.d.*, 1845

*Deleted from sketch; see 96:18–97:3:*

(3) inexplicable.
      Death cannot explain itself. The earnestness consists precisely in this, that the observer himself must explain it to himself.
                              —*Pap.* VI B 120:13 *n.d.*, 1845

*Deleted from sketch; see 96:18–97:3:*

VI
B 120:6
210

. . . . . whether it gladdens or saddens one, death does not know.

if it helps someone contemplating suicide from becoming a suicide—or carries someone away in the most beautiful moment

VI
B 120:6
211

If you saw him, the pale, grim harvester, stand idle and lean on his scythe, and you would then go up to him, whether you thought your boredom with life would curry favor with him or your burning longing for the eternal would move him if you laid your hand on his shoulder and said, "Explain yourself." Do you think he would reply; I think he would not even notice that you put your hand on his shoulder.
—*Pap.* VI B 120:6 *n.d.*, 1845

*Deleted from sketch; see 97:29–98:29:*

Death inexplicable. The unity of being the most earnest and nothing, that is, irony and humor, but it is mood—or comes as the final good fortune, which reconciles everything.—*Pap.* VI B 120:14 *n.d.*, 1845

*From draft; see 98:20:*

He perhaps lived for a long time in youthful confidence in life; then he believed in someone, and see, he was deceived, and see, he was deceived again; then the childishness within him concentrated upon death, and death . . . . . . —*Pap.* VI B 124:1 *n.d.*, 1845

*From sketch; see 98:38–100:30:*

. . . . . the last of all.
Suffering—Metamorphosis—Transition
Each one of these expressions contains a whole life-view. It is easy to recite them all, but the uncertainty of death will

of course make an inspection to see whether one is living accordingly.—*Pap.* VI B 120:15 *n.d.*, 1845

*From draft; see 99:19:*

. . . . . so he sees that after all it is mood, [*deleted:* about everything else one can unabashedly have an opinion] and that the one explaining, despite his profound opinion, has not even grasped the qualification of the uncertainty of death.—*Pap.* VI B 124:2 *n.d.*, 1845

*From sketch; see 99:29–100:27:*

About everything else one can quite unabashedly have an opinion, about a remote event, about nature, etc., but about death it is dangerous, because at that very same moment the uncertainty of death makes an inspection to see whether one's life actually expresses this explanation and this opinion. And if one has no conception of the uncertainty of death, then what opinion one has is of little avail.—*Pap.* VI B 120:21 *n.d.*, 1845

*From sketch; see 100:28–34:*

Therefore the discourse will give no explanation, but the inexplicability of death will be the last, just as death itself is the last, the boundary that provides retroactive power so that it is over and its decision is indefinable.—*Pap.* VI B 120:22 *n.d.*, 1845

*From sketch; see 101:3–21:*

Conclusion
in a mitigating tone.
—*Pap.* VI B 120:7 *n.d.*, 1845

*From draft; see 101:4:*

. . . . . but you bear in mind also that to know a great deal is not an unconditional good, and that one is helped to the one

VI
B 124:3
215

thing needful—[*deleted:* appropriation] the possession of that
incorruptible property that moth and rust cannot consume[54]
nor sickness and adversity disturb—also in this way, by dwelling on the thought about how one knows it.—*Pap.* VI B
124:3 *n.d.*, 1845

*Penciled in draft; see 102:15–29:*

. . . . . and who in uncertainty is always at your service,
and finally holds the examination.
                                                    —*Pap.* VI B 124:4 *n.d.*, 1845

*From* The Book on Adler; *see 5:5:*

Note. One or another reader perhaps recalls that I have always used this expression about myself *qua* author, that I am
*without authority*, and have used it so emphatically that it *has
been repeated as a formula in every preface.*[55] Even though as an
author I have had no benefit, I have at least done everything
finitely possible not to confuse the highest and the holiest. I am
a poor individual human being. If I am, as some think, a bit of a
genius, about that I would say: Let it go hang. But an apostle is
in all eternity qualitatively just as different from me as from the
greatest genius who has ever lived and from the most obtuse
person who has ever lived.—*Pap.* VII² B 235, p. 144 *n.d.*,
1846–47

# EDITORIAL APPENDIX

# ACKNOWLEDGMENTS

Preparation of manuscripts for *Kierkegaard's Writings* is supported by a genuinely enabling grant from the National Endowment for the Humanities. The grant includes gifts from the Dronning Margrethes og Prins Henriks Fond, the Danish Ministry of Cultural Affairs, the Augustinus Fond, the Carlsberg Fond, and the Lutheran Brotherhood Foundation.

The translators-editors are indebted to Grethe Kjær and Julia Watkin for their knowledgeable observations on crucial concepts and terminology and their critical reading of the text.

Per Lønning, Wim R. Scholtens, and Sophia Scopetéa, members of the International Advisory Board for *Kierkegaard's Writings*, gave valuable criticism of the manuscript on the whole and in detail. Jack Schwandt helpfully read the entire manuscript. Kathryn Hong and Regine Prenzel-Guthrie, associate editors of *KW*, scrutinized the manuscript, and Regine Prenzel-Guthrie prepared the index.

Acknowledgment is made to Gyldendals Forlag for permission to absorb notes to *Søren Kierkegaards samlede Værker*.

Inclusion in the Supplement of entries from *Søren Kierkegaard's Journals and Papers* is by arrangement with Indiana University Press.

The book collection and the microfilm collection of the Kierkegaard Library, St. Olaf College, and Gregor Malantschuk's annotated set of *Kierkegaards samlede Værker* have been used in preparation of the text, Supplement, and Editorial Appendix.

Word processing of the manuscript and preparation of the composition tape were done by Francesca Lane Rasmus. The volume has been guided through the press by Marta Steele.

# COLLATION OF *THREE DISCOURSES ON IMAGINED OCCASIONS* IN THE DANISH EDITIONS OF KIERKEGAARD'S COLLECTED WORKS

| Vol. V Ed. 1 Pg. | Vol. V Ed. 2 Pg. | Vol. 6 Ed. 3 Pg. | Vol. V Ed. 1 Pg. | Vol. V Ed. 2 Pg. | Vol. 6 Ed. 3 Pg. |
|---|---|---|---|---|---|
| 175 | 199 | 245 | 207 | 237 | 277 |
| 177 | 201 | 247 | 208 | 238 | 278 |
| 178 | 202 | 247 | 209 | 240 | 279 |
| 179 | 203 | 248 | 210 | 241 | 280 |
| 180 | 204 | 249 | 211 | 242 | 281 |
| 181 | 205 | 250 | 212 | 243 | 282 |
| 182 | 206 | 251 | 213 | 245 | 283 |
| 183 | 207 | 252 | 214 | 246 | 284 |
| 184 | 209 | 253 | 215 | 247 | 285 |
| 185 | 210 | 254 | 216 | 248 | 286 |
| 186 | 211 | 255 | 217 | 250 | 287 |
| 187 | 212 | 256 | 218 | 251 | 288 |
| 188 | 214 | 258 | 219 | 252 | 289 |
| 189 | 215 | 259 | 220 | 253 | 290 |
| 190 | 216 | 260 | 221 | 255 | 291 |
| 191 | 217 | 261 | 222 | 256 | 292 |
| 192 | 219 | 262 | 223 | 257 | 293 |
| 193 | 220 | 263 | 224 | 258 | 294 |
| 194 | 221 | 264 | 225 | 260 | 295 |
| 195 | 222 | 265 | 226 | 261 | 296 |
| 196 | 224 | 266 | 227 | 262 | 296 |
| 197 | 225 | 267 | 228 | 263 | 297 |
| 198 | 226 | 268 | 229 | 264 | 298 |
| 199 | 227 | 269 | 230 | 265 | 299 |
| 200 | 229 | 270 | 231 | 266 | 300 |
| 201 | 230 | 271 | 232 | 268 | 301 |
| 202 | 231 | 272 | 233 | 269 | 302 |
| 203 | 232 | 273 | 234 | 270 | 303 |
| 204 | 234 | 274 | 235 | 271 | 304 |
| 205 | 235 | 274 | 236 | 272 | 305 |
| 206 | 236 | 275 | 237 | 274 | 306 |

| *Vol. V* | *Vol. V* | *Vol. 6* | *Vol. V* | *Vol. V* | *Vol. 6* |
|---|---|---|---|---|---|
| *Ed. 1* | *Ed. 2* | *Ed. 3* | *Ed. 1* | *Ed. 2* | *Ed. 3* |
| *Pg.* | *Pg.* | *Pg.* | *Pg.* | *Pg.* | *Pg.* |
| 238 | 275 | 307 | 246 | 285 | 316 |
| 239 | 276 | 309 | 247 | 286 | 317 |
| 240 | 277 | 310 | 248 | 287 | 318 |
| 241 | 279 | 311 | 249 | 288 | 319 |
| 242 | 280 | 312 | 250 | 290 | 320 |
| 243 | 281 | 313 | 251 | 291 | 321 |
| 244 | 282 | 314 | 252 | 292 | 322 |
| 245 | 284 | 315 | 253 | 293 | 323 |

# NOTES

TITLE

*Three Discourses.* See Supplement, pp. 126–27 (*Pap.* VI B 138, 100, 125:1,2).

## PREFACE

See Supplement, pp. 127–30, 152 (*Pap.* VI B 140, 141, 142, 159, A 25; VI B 101, 102, 103; VII² B 235, p. 144).
*occasion.* See Supplement, p. 127 (*Pap.* VI B 142).
*authority.* See Supplement, p. 152 (*Pap.* VII² B 235, p. 144).

## ON THE OCCASION OF A CONFESSION

1. See Supplement, pp. 130–31 (*Pap.* VI B 139, 143).
2. With reference to the following paragraph, see Supplement, pp. 131–33 (*Pap.* VI B 161, 164, 150).
3. With reference to the following sentence, see Supplement, p. 133 (*Pap.* VI B 180).
4. See Matthew 19:24; Mark 10:25.
5. See Matthew 6:6.
6. See Supplement, p. 133 (*Pap.* VI B 125:5).
7. See II Corinthians 6:10. See Supplement, pp. 133–34 (*Pap.* VI B 157).
8. See John 11:4.
9. With reference to the following five paragraphs, see Supplement, p. 134 (*Pap.* VI B 104:1).
10. The Danish *Bedested* literally means "place of prayer" and by extension "biding place" or "rest stop" on a journey.
11. See Romans 3:19.
12. See Job 9:3.
13. See Matthew 5:25.
14. With reference to the following three sentences, see Supplement, p. 134 (*Pap.* VI B 106:2).
15. Julius Caesar. See Plutarch, "Caesar," 54, "Cato Minor," 72, *Lives*; *Plutarchi vitae parallelae*, I–IX, ed. G. H. Schaefer (Leipzig: 1829; *ASKB* 1181–89), VII, pp. 64, 213; *Plutarch's Lives*, I–XI, tr. Bernadotte Perrin (Loeb, Cambridge: Harvard University Press, 1968–84), VII, pp. 568–69; VIII, pp. 408–09.
16. The source has not been located.
17. See Lessing, *Minna von Barnhelm*, II, 7; *Gotthold Ephraim Lessing's sämmtliche Schriften*, I–XXXII (Berlin, Stettin: 1825–28; *ASKB* 1747–62), XX, p.

241; *Laocoön, Nathan the Wise, Minna von Barnhelm*, tr. William A. Steel (Everyman, New York: Dent, 1930), p. 245: "One thankful thought to Heaven is the best of prayers!" See also *JP* IV 4364 (*Pap.* VI A 2).

18. See, for example, *Fragments*, p. 39, *KW* VII (*SV* IV 207).

19. See, for example, ibid., pp. 80–81, 86 (244, 250).

20. For continuation of the sentence and also with reference to the following two sentences, see Supplement, p. 134 (*Pap.* VI B 104:3).

21. With reference to the following seven sentences, see Supplement, p. 135 (*Pap.* VI B 104:4).

22. Cf. *The Point of View for my Work as an Author*, in *The Point of View*, *KW* XXII (*SV* XIII 527).

23. With reference to the following paragraph, see Supplement, p. 135 (*Pap.* VI B 105).

24. Cf. Psalm 139:7.

25. Cf., for example, *Fragments*, pp. 39–44, *KW* VII (*SV* IV 207–11).

26. With reference to the remainder of the paragraph and the following two sentences, see Supplement, p. 135 (*Pap.* VI B 108:2).

27. Cf. *JP* V 5100, pp. 34–35 (*Pap.* I A 75, pp. 53–54).

28. See Exodus 7:10–12.

29. With reference to the following sentence, see Supplement, p. 135 (*Pap.* VI B 108:3).

30. See, for example, Xenophon, *Memorabilia*, II, 1, 20; *Xenophontis opera graece et latine*, I-IV, ed. Karl August Thieme (Leipzig: 1801–04; *ASKB* 1207–10), IV, p. 73; *Xenophontis memorabilia*, ed. Friedrich August Bornemann (Leipzig: 1829), p. 90; *Xenophons Sokratiske Merkværdigheder*, tr. Jens Bloch (Copenhagen: 1802), p. 118; *Xenophon, Memorabilia and Oeconomicus*, tr. E. C. Marchant (Loeb, Cambridge: Harvard University Press, 1979), pp. 92–93:

And so says Hesiod somewhere [*Works and Days*, 285]:

"Wickedness can be had in abundance easily: smooth is the road and very nigh she dwells. But in front of virtue the gods immortal have put sweat: long and steep is the path to her and rough at first; but when you reach the top, then at length the road is easy, hard though it was."

31. Cf. Romans 3:5, 6:1.

32. With reference to the remainder of the paragraph, see Supplement, p. 136 (*Pap.* VI B 108:4). See also *Point of View*, *KW* XXII (*SV* XIII 571).

33. With reference to the remainder of the paragraph, see Supplement, p. 136 (*Pap.* VI B 108:5).

34. See Matthew 6:17.

35. Cf. Matthew 7:13–14.

36. Cf. *Practice in Christianity*, pp. 233–34, *KW* XX (*SV* XII 213–14).

37. For continuation of the paragraph, see Supplement, p. 136 (*Pap.* VI B 108:7).

38. See Supplement, p. 136 (*Pap.* VI B 125:7).

39. For continuation of the paragraph, see Supplement, p. 137 (*Pap.* VI B 125:8).

40. See John 8:1–11.

41. Cf. Hans Adolph Brorson, *"I denne søde Juletid,"* stanza 6, *Psalmer og aandelige Sange*, ed. Jens Albrecht Leonhard Holm (Copenhagen: 1838; *ASKB* 200), 9, p. 28.

42. See Matthew 25:21; Luke 16:10–11.

43. See p. 49. See also Supplement, p. 135 (*Pap.* VI B 108:10); J. Ewald, *Fiskerne*, III, 4, *Johannes Ewalds samtlige Skrifter*, I–IV (Copenhagen: 1780–91; *ASKB* 1533–36), III, p. 233.

44. See Supplement, p. 137 (*Pap.* VI B 108:11).

45. See II Corinthians 12:7.

46. Socrates and his daimon. See, for example, Xenophon, *Memorabilia*, I, 1, 2; *Opera*, IV, p. 2; Bornemann, p. 3; Bloch, p. 3; Loeb, pp. 2–3.

## ON THE OCCASION OF A WEDDING

1. Danish has two words for love: *Elskov* and *Kjærlighed*. *Elskov* pertains to love between man and woman and may be translated as "erotic love" or "romantic love." *Kjærlighed* has a wider and deeper meaning. The distinction between the two is not unlike that between *eros* and *agape*.

2. Cf. Genesis 3:16–19.

3. See Supplement, p. 137 (*Pap.* VI B 125:9).

4. At that time, the pastor officiating at a wedding received an established fee.

5. See Plato, *Symposium*, 178 a–c; *Platonis quae exstant opera*, I–XI, ed. Friederich Ast (Leipzig: 1819–32; *ASKB* 1144–54), III, pp. 444–45; *Udvalgte Dialoger af Platon*, I–VIII, tr. Carl Johan Heise (Copenhagen: 1830–59; *ASKB* 1164–67, 1169 [I–VII]), II, p. 15; *The Collected Dialogues of Plato*, ed. Edith Hamilton and Huntington Cairns (Princeton: Princeton University Press, 1963), pp. 532–33 (Socrates speaking):

> As I was saying, then, Phaedrus opened with some such arguments as these—that Love was a great god, wonderful alike to the gods and to mankind, and that of all the proofs of this the greatest was his birth.
>
> The worship of this god, he said, is of the oldest, for Love is unbegotten, nor is there mention of his parentage to be found anywhere in either prose or verse, while Hesiod tells us expressly that Chaos first appeared, and then
>
> From Chaos rose broad-bosomed Earth, the sure
> And everlasting seat of all that is,
> And after, Love . . . [*Theogony*, 116–19]
>
> Acusilaus agrees with Hesiod, for he holds that after Chaos were brought forth these twain, Earth and Love, and Parmenides writes of the creative principle.
>
> And Love she framed the first of all the gods [*Parmenides*, 13].
>
> Thus we find that the antiquity of Love is universally admitted, and in very truth he is the ancient source of all our highest good.

6. I Timothy 6:12.

7. See Ecclesiastes 12:1.

8. See I Corinthians 13:1.

9. See, for example, "Against Cowardliness," *Eighteen Discourses*, p. 347, *KW* V (*SV* V 124).

10. With reference to the remainder of the paragraph, see Supplement, pp. 137–38 (*Pap.* VI B 112:1). See also p. 37 and note 43.

11. Cf. *Repetition*, pp. 135–36, *KW* VI (*SV* III 177–78); *JP* I 804 (*Pap.* III A 95).

12. See Luke 7:47.

13. Cf. Matthew 6:2,5,6,16.

14. See I Corinthians 9:26.

15. See Romans 4:18. See also, for example, *For Self-Examination*, pp. 82–83, *KW* XXI (*SV* XII 365–66).

16. See Psalm 126:5.

17. With reference to the remainder of the paragraph and the following paragraph, see Supplement, p. 138 (*Pap.* VI B 112:2).

18. Danish: *Hvedebrødsdage*, "wheat-bread days," in contrast to the ordinary days with a fare of bread made from whole rye or unsifted rye.

19. With reference to the following sentence, see Supplement, p. 139 (*Pap.* VI B 113:1).

20. With reference to the following paragraph, see Supplement, p. 139 (*Pap.* VI B 113:2).

21. With reference to the following sentence, see Supplement, p. 139 (*Pap.* VI B 113:3).

22. With reference to the following sentence, see Supplement, p. 139 (*Pap.* VI B 113:4).

23. With reference to the remainder of the paragraph, see Supplement, pp. 139–40 (*Pap.* VI B 113:5,6).

24. With reference to the remainder of the paragraph, see Supplement, p. 140 (*Pap.* VI B 113:8). Cf. *Either/Or*, II, pp. 161–63, 176–78, 213–16, *KW* IV (*SV* II 147–49, 160–61, 191–94).

25. With reference to the following paragraph, see Supplement, p. 140 (*Pap.* VI B 114:1).

26. With reference to the following three sentences, see Supplement, p. 140 (*Pap.* VI B 114:2).

27. With reference to the following paragraph, see Supplement, pp. 140–41 (*Pap.* VI B 114:3).

28. See Philippians 2:12.

29. See John 2:1–11.

30. With reference to the following ten paragraphs, see Supplement, pp. 141–43 (*Pap.* VI B 118).

31. Cf. Matthew 25:1–13.

### AT A GRAVESIDE

1. With reference to the following fourteen paragraphs, see Supplement, p. 143 (*Pap.* VI B 144).

2. On Kierkegaard's distinction between remembering and recollecting, see *Stages*, pp. 9–15, *KW* XI (*SV* VI 15–20).

3. See Psalm 6:5.

4. See Psalm 56:3.

5. With reference to the remainder of the paragraph and the following seven paragraphs, see Supplement, pp. 143–45 (*Pap.* VI B 120:1, 179).

6. See, for example, *Stages*, p. 28, *KW* XI (*SV* VI 31).

7. Epicurus. See Diogenes Laertius, *Lives of Eminent Philosophers*, X, 125; *Diogenis Laertii de vitis philosophorum libri X*, I–II (Leipzig: 1833; *ASKB* 1109), II, p. 235; *Diogen Laërtses filosofiske Historie*, I–II, tr. Børge Riisbrigh (Copenhagen: 1812; *ASKB* 1110–11), I, p. 502; *Diogenes Laertius, Lives of Eminent Philosophers*, I–II, tr. R. D. Hicks (Loeb, Cambridge: Harvard University Press, 1979–80), II, pp. 650–51:

> Accustom thyself to believe that death is nothing to us, for good and evil imply sentience, and death is the privation of all sentience; therefore a right understanding that death is nothing to us makes the mortality of life enjoyable, not by adding to life an illimitable time, but by taking away the yearning after immortality. For life has no terrors for him who has thoroughly apprehended that there are no terrors for him in ceasing to live. Foolish, therefore, is the man who says that he fears death, not because it will pain when it comes, but because it pains in the prospect. Whatsoever causes no annoyance when it is present, causes only a groundless pain in the expectation. Death, therefore, the most awful of evils, is nothing to us, seeing that, when we are, death is not come, and, when death is come, we are not. It is nothing, then, either to the living or to the dead, for with the living it is not and the dead exist no longer.

8. With reference to the following three paragraphs, see Supplement, p. 144 (*Pap.* VI B 119:1).

9. A supplication in the Litany, a form of prayer used as early as the fifth century. See, for example, *The Book of Common Prayer* (New York: Seabury, 1976), p. 54:

> From lightning and tempest; from earthquake, fire, and flood; from plague, pestilence, and famine; from battle and murder, and from sudden death,
> *Good Lord, deliver us.*

For an explanation of the phrase "sudden death," see Marion J. Hatchett, *Commentary on the American Prayer Book* (New York: Seabury, 1980), p. 160:

> For over three hundred years the petition to be delivered "from sudden death" has been criticized as misleading. In the medieval litany the petition asked that we be delivered from an unexpected death—one for which we were not prepared. The phrase "from dying suddenly and unprepared" replaces "from sudden death" in this revision.

10. Cf., for example, "to die death," *The Sickness unto Death*, p. 18, *KW* XIX (*SV* XI 132).

11. With reference to the remainder of the sentence and the following paragraph, see Supplement, p. 144 (*Pap.* VI B 119:3).

12. With reference to the following paragraph, see Supplement, pp. 143–45 (*Pap.* VI B 120:1, 179).

13. See Jean Paul (Johann Paul Friedrich Richter), *Jean Paul's Briefe und bevorstehender Lebenslauf, Briefe 4, "An Benigna, Postskript: Die Neujahrnacht eines Unglücklichen," Jean Paul's sämmtliche Werke,* I-LX (Berlin: 1826–28; *ASKB* 1777–99), XXXV, pp. 46–48. See Supplement, pp. 143–45 (*Pap.* VI B 120:1, 179).

14. Emperor Karl V (1500–1558) of Germany. According to disputed reports, before his death in the San Juste monastery in Estramadura, Spain, he had a practice burial. See Supplement, pp. 143–45 (*Pap.* VI B 120:1, 179).

15. With reference to the remainder of the paragraph, see Supplement, p. 144 (*Pap.* VI B 119:4).

16. Cf. Matthew 10:28.

17. See Ephesians 2:12.

18. With reference to the following two paragraphs, see Supplement, p. 145 (*Pap.* VI B 120:18). With reference to the following three paragraphs, see Supplement, p. 145 (*Pap.* VI B 120:10).

19. With reference to the remainder of the paragraph, see Supplement, p. 145 (*Pap.* VI B 145).

20. With reference to the following two sentences, see Supplement, p. 146 (*Pap.* VI B 120:2).

21. See Job 38:11.

22. With reference to the remainder of the paragraph, see Supplement, p. 146 (*Pap.* VI B 178, 120:19).

23. With reference to the following sentence, see Supplement, p. 146 (*Pap.* VI B 120:9).

24. See Supplement, p. 146 (*Pap.* VI B 125:10).

25. With reference to the remainder of the paragraph and the following two paragraphs, see Supplement, p. 147 (*Pap.* VI B 120:3).

26. With reference to the remainder of the sentence, see Supplement, p. 147 (*Pap.* VI B 122:1).

27. See John 9:4.

28. See Supplement, p. 147 (*Pap.* VI B 125:11).

29. See Isaiah 22:13; I Corinthians 15:32.

30. See I Thessalonians 5:2.

31. See John 9:4.

32. With reference to the following twelve pages, see Supplement, pp. 147–48 (*Pap.* VI B 120:4, 120:11).

33. With reference to the following two paragraphs, see Supplement, p. 148 (*Pap.* VI B 120:12).

34. Cf. *Sickness unto Death*, p. 74, *KW* XIX (*SV* XI 184–85).

35. Cf. Shakespeare, *Hamlet*, V, 1; *William Shakspeare's Tragiske Værker,* I-IX, tr. Peter Foersom and Peter Frederik Wulff (Copenhagen: 1807–25;

*ASKB* 1889–96), I, pp. 193–95; *W. Shakspeare's dramatische Werke*, I-VIII, tr. Ernst Ortlepp (Stuttgart: 1838–39; *ASKB* 1874–81), I, pp. 360–61; *Shakspeare's dramatische Werke*, I-XII, tr. August Wilhelm v. Schlegel and Ludwig Tieck (Berlin: 1839–40; *ASKB* 1883–88), VI, pp. 121–22; *The Complete Works of Shakespeare*, ed. George Lyman Kittredge (Boston: Ginn, 1936), p. 1186.

36. With reference to the remainder of the sentence, see Supplement, p. 148 (*Pap.* VI B 122:2).

37. With reference to the remainder of the sentence, see Supplement, p. 148 (*Pap.* VI B 122:3). Cf. Homer, *Odyssey*, XI, 487–91; *Homers Odyssee*, I-II, tr. Christian Wilster (Copenhagen: 1837), I, p. 160; *Homer, The Odyssey*, I-II, tr. A. T. Murray (Loeb, Cambridge: Harvard University Press, 1976–80), I, pp. 420–21:

> "So I [Odysseus] spoke, and he [Achilles] straightway made answer and said: 'Nay, seek not to speak soothingly to me of death, glorious Odysseus. I should choose, so I might live on earth, to serve as the hireling of another, of some portionless man whose livelihood was but small, rather than to be lord over all the dead that have perished.'"

38. With reference to the remainder of the paragraph, see Supplement, p. 148 (*Pap.* VI B 122:4).

39. See I Thessalonians 5:3.

40. See Luke 12:16–20.

41. See Matthew 6:31–32.

42. Cf., for example, *The Concept of Anxiety*, pp. 30, 32, 129–32, *KW* VIII (*SV* IV 303, 304, 396–99).

43. With reference to the remainder of the paragraph, see Supplement, p. 149 (*Pap.* VI B 122:5).

44. With reference to the remainder of the paragraph, see Supplement, p. 149 (*Pap.* VI B 122:6).

45. See Matthew 3:10.

46. With reference to the remainder of the sentence and the following sentence, see Supplement, p. 149 (*Pap.* VI B 122:7).

47. An allusion to Solon and Croesus. See, for example, Herodotus, *History*, I, 32, 34, 86; *Die Geschichten des Herodotos*, I-II, tr. Friedrich Lange (Berlin: 1811–12; *ASKB* 1117), I, pp. 18–19, 20, 49–50; *Herodotus*, I-IV, tr. A. D. Godley (Loeb, Cambridge: Harvard University Press, 1981–82), I, pp. 38–39, 40–41, 108–11:

> Thus then, Croesus, the whole of man is but chance. Now if I am to speak of you, I say that I see you very rich and the king of many men. But I cannot yet answer your question, before I hear that you have ended your life well. . . . If then such a man besides all this shall also end his life well, then he is the man whom you seek, and is worthy to be called blest; but we must wait till he be dead, and call him not yet blest, but fortunate.

But after Solon's departure, the divine anger fell heavily on Croesus: as I guess, because he supposed himself to be blest beyond all other men.

So the Persians took Sardis and made Croesus himself prisoner, he having reigned fourteen years and been besieged fourteen days, and, as the oracle foretold, brought his own great empire to an end. Having then taken him they led him to Cyrus. Cyrus had a great pyre built, on which he set Croesus, bound in chains, and twice seven Lydian boys beside him: either his intent was to sacrifice these first-fruits to some one of his gods, or he desired to fulfil a vow, or it may be that, learning that Croesus was a god-fearing man, he set him for this cause on the pyre, because he would fain know if any deity would save him from being burnt alive. It is related then that he did this; but Croesus, as he stood on the pyre, remembered even in his evil plight how divinely inspired was that saying of Solon, that no living man was blest. When this came to his mind, having till now spoken no word, he sighed deeply and groaned, and thrice uttered the name of Solon. Cyrus heard it, and bade his interpreters ask Croesus who was this on whom he called; they came near and asked him; Croesus at first would say nothing in answer, but presently, being compelled, he said, "It is one with whom I would have given much wealth that all sovereigns should hold converse." This was a dark saying to them, and again they questioned him of the words which he spoke. As they were instant, and troubled him, he told them then how Solon, an Athenian, had first come, and how he had seen all his royal state and made light of it (saying thus and thus), and how all had happened to Croesus as Solon said, though he spoke with less regard to Croesus than to mankind in general and chiefly those who deemed themselves blest. While Croesus thus told his story, the pyre had already been kindled and the outer parts of it were burning. Then Cyrus, when he heard from the interpreters what Croesus said, repented of his purpose.

48. With reference to the following two paragraphs, see Supplement, pp. 149–50 (*Pap.* VI B 120:5, 120:13, 120:6).

49. With reference to the remainder of the paragraph, see Supplement, p. 150 (*Pap.* VI B 120:6).

50. See James 1:19.

51. With reference to the following two paragraphs, see Supplement, p. 150 (*Pap.* VI B 120:14).

52. For continuation of the text, see Supplement, p. 150 (*Pap.* VI B 124:1).

53. With reference to the following four paragraphs and the following two sentences, see Supplement, pp. 150–51 (*Pap.* VI B 120:15).

54. See Romans 6:23.

55. For continuation of the sentence, see Supplement, p. 150 (*Pap.* VI B 124:2).

56. With reference to the following two paragraphs, see Supplement, p. 150 (*Pap.* VI B 120:21).

57. Cf. *Postscript*, pp. 194–96, *KW* XII.1 (*SV* VII 162–63).

58. With reference to the following three sentences, see Supplement, p. 151 (*Pap.* VI B 120:22).

59. With reference to the following paragraph, see Supplement, p. 151 (*Pap.* VI B 120:7).

60. For continuation of the sentence, see Supplement, pp. 151–52 (*Pap.* VI B 124:3).

61. Presumably an allusion to Bishop Jakob Peter Mynster. See Supplement, pp. 135, 141–43 (*Pap.* VI B 108:3, 118).

62. With reference to the remainder of the paragraph, see Supplement, p. 152 (*Pap.* VI B 124:4).

**SUPPLEMENT**

1. See Genesis 4:10.

2. See Aristotle, *Categories*, 2 a-3 a; *Aristoteles graece*, I-II, ed. Immanuel Bekker (Berlin: 1831; *ASKB* 1074–75), I, pp. 2–3; *The Complete Works of Aristotle*, I-II, ed. Jonathan Barnes (rev. Oxford tr., Princeton: Princeton University Press, 1984), I, pp. 4–6.

3. See Aristotle, *Rhetoric*, 1354 a, 1355 a; Bekker, II, pp. 1354–55; *Works*, II, pp. 2152–54.

4. See *JP* I 630, 631; II 1116, 1467; III 3192, 3467–71; V 5786 (*Pap.* VI A 146–56).

5. Heinrich Ritter, *Geschichte der Philosophie*, I-VIII (Hamburg: 1836–45; *ASKB* 735–38 [I-IV]); *The History of Ancient Philosophy*, I-IV, tr. Alexander J. W. Morrison (Oxford: 1838–46), III, pp. 617–19.

6. See *JP* II 2281 (*Pap.* IV C 23).

7. See Aristotle, *Rhetoric*, 1355 a, 1356 b, 1358 a, 1395 b-1397 a; Bekker, II, pp. 1355, 1356, 1358, 1395–97; *Works*, II, pp. 2153–54, 2156, 2158–59, 2224–25.

8. The projected work on religious discourse. See Supplement, pp. 110–11, 119–25 (*Pap.* VI A 17, 19, B 131, 133).

9. See Proverbs 10:7; *Postscript*, pp. 235–36, *KW* XII.1 (*SV* VII 198). See also Supplement, pp. 109–10 (*Pap.* V A 36, 56).

10. Jens Finsteen Gi(j)ødwad (1811–1891), editor of *Fædrelandet* and Kierkegaard's middleman in the publication of the early pseudonymous works.

11. Peder Hansen (1798–1880), governor of the Danish East Indies 1841–1847.

12. See Shakespeare, *Twelfth Night*, II, 4; *Hellig Tre Kongers Aften, eller Hvad man vil*, tr. Adolphe Engelbert Boye, *Det Kongelige Theaters Repertoire*, I-VI (Copenhagen: 1828–42), I, 22 (1829), p. 13; *W. Shakspeare's dramatische Werke*, I-VIII, tr. Ernst Ortlepp (Stuttgart: 1838–39; *ASKB* 1874–81), III, p. 472; *Shakspeare's dramatische Werke*, I-XII, tr. August Wilhelm v. Schlegel and Ludwig Tieck (Berlin 1839–40; *ASKB* 1883–88, V, 139); *The Complete Works of Shakespeare*, ed. George Lyman Kittredge (Boston: Ginn, 1936), p. 412:

DUKE: What dost thou know?

VIOLA: Too well what love women to men may owe.
In faith, they are as true of heart as we.
My father had a daughter lov'd a man
As it might be perhaps, were I a woman,
I should your lordship.

DUKE: And what's her history?

VIOLA: A blank, my lord. She never told her love,
But let concealment, like a worm i' th' bud,
Feed on her damask cheek. She pin'd in thought;
And, with a green and yellow melancholy,
She sat like Patience on a monument,
Smiling at grief. Was not this love indeed?

13. Matthew 11:28.

14. See Luke 2:36–38.

15. See Matthew 6:25.

16. Napoleon. See Adolphe Thiers, *Den franske Revolutions Historie*, I-VII, tr. Frederik Carl Rosen (Copenhagen: 1842–45), VII, p. 291; *Geschichte der französischen Revolution*, I-V, tr. Ferdinand Philippi (Leipzig: 1836; *ASKB* 2024–28), V, p. 318. See also *Postscript*, p. 355, *KW* XII.1 (*SV* VII 308).

17. See Mark 14:66–72; Luke 22:54–62.

18. See Matthew 15:22–28.

19. See note 17 above.

20. See Diogenes Laertius, *Lives of Eminent Philosophers*, II, 35; *Diogenis Laertii de vitis philosophorum libri X*, I-II (Leipzig: 1833; *ASKB* 1109), I, p. 77; *Diogen Laërtses filosofiske Historie*, I-II, tr. Børge Riisbrigh (Copenhagen: 1812; *ASKB* 1110–11), I, p. 72; *Diogenes Laertius*, I-II, tr. R. D. Hicks (Loeb, Cambridge: Harvard University Press, 1979–80), I, pp. 164–65: "When his wife said, 'You suffer unjustly,' he retorted, 'Why, would you have me suffer justly?'"

21. Cf. Luke 23:41. The Danish text has "guilty [*skyldig*]," but it presumably should read "innocent [*uskyldig*]"; see Supplement, p. 116 (*Pap.* VI B 170). See also, for example, *Discourses in Various Spirits*, pp. 281–82, *KW* XV (*SV* VIII 364).

22. See Joel 2:12.

23. Grecian fire was a combustible material capable of burning under water and was used by the ancient Greek navy. Old books on fireworks have formulae for Grecian fire. See *JP* IV 4008 (*Pap.* VI A 30).

24. See *JP* II 1989 (*Pap.* VI A 20).

25. See Matthew 11:16–17.

26. See Matthew 9:21.

27. The projected work on religious discourse that was intended to accompany ("not bound into the volume") *Discourses on Imagined Occasions*. See Historical Introduction, pp. viii–ix; Supplement, pp. 110–12, 119–26 (*Pap.* VI A 17, 19, B 131, 132, 133, 137).

28. The pseudonymous author of *Fear and Trembling, KW* VI (*SV* III).

29. See I Corinthians 9:24–27.

30. D. Th. Balthasar Münter, curate of Holmens Church, preached on I Corinthians 9:24–10:6, the text for Septuagesima Sunday, January 19, 1845.

31. See *JP* V 5781, 5782 (*Pap.* VI C 4, 5).

32. See Supplement, p. 111 (*Pap.* VI A 147).

33. See *JP* II 1291 (*Pap.* VI A 21).

34. Bishop Jakob Peter Mynster. The pseudonym Kts is formed from the initial consonant in the second syllable of each name. See, for example, "An Explanation and a Little More," in Corsair *Affair*, p. 26, *KW* XIII (*SV* XIII 421); *Stages*, pp. 649–51, *KW* XI (*Pap.* VI B 184); *Fear and Trembling*, pp. xxxvi–xxxvii, *KW* VI; *Pap.* VI B 98:52.

35. Johan Nicolai Madvig (1804–1886), Latin scholar and frequent writer of reviews. See Corsair *Affair*, p. 26, *KW* XIII (*SV* XIII 421).

36. Cf. *JP* V 5740 (*Pap.* V A 58).

37. Drinking pledge of lifelong friendship. See Ludvig Holberg, *Mester Gert Westphaler eller Den meget talende Barbeer*, 8, *Den Danske Skue-Plads*, I–VII (Copenhagen: 1788; *ASKB* 1566–67), I, no pagination; *Seven One-Act Plays by Holberg*, tr. Henry Alexander (Princeton: Princeton University Press, 1950), p. 30.

38. See *Postscript*, p. 103, *KW* XII.1 (*SV* VII 83).

39. See Ludvig Holberg, *Erasmus Montanus eller Rasmus Berg*, I, 3, *Danske Skue-Plads*, V, no pagination; *Comedies by Holberg*, tr. Oscar James Campbell, Jr., and Frederic Schenck (New York: American-Scandinavian Foundation, 1935), p. 124.

40. For continuation of the paragraph, see Supplement, pp. 125–26 (*Pap.* VI B 137).

41. Christian Winther, *Sang og Sagn* (Copenhagen: 1840).

42. Cf. "An Occasional Discourse," *Discourses in Various Spirits*, p. 5, *KW* XV (*SV* VIII 117).

43. See note 42 above.

44. See note 42 above.

45. Cf. Matthew 5:8.

46. See II Corinthians 7:10.

47. See "An Occasional Discourse," *Discourses in Various Spirits*, pp. 86, 94, *KW* XV (*SV* VIII 185, 192).

48. Bishop Mynster (see note 34 above) preached in the Slotskirke on the Epistle II Corinthians 6:1–10.

49. See II Corinthians 6:10.

50. Presumably the two verbs were intended to be reversed: "Someone who had everything and yet possessed nothing."

51. Bishop Jakob Peter Mynster, *Prædikener af Dr. J. P. Mynster*, I–II (Copenhagen: 1826–32; *ASKB* 228). In 1802 Mynster became pastor at Spj(i)ellerup and Smerup. The period there (1802–1811) was of decisive

ethical-religious significance for Mynster. The collection of sermons published in 1810 is known as the "Spjellerup sermons."

52. See Mynster, *Prædikener,* I, p. 276.

53. See Supplement, pp. 135, 136 (*Pap.* VI B 108:3,7, 125:7).

54. See Matthew 6:19–20.

55. See *Two Upbuilding Discourses* (1843): "Its author does not have authority," *Eighteen Discourses,* p. 5, *KW* V (*SV* III 11). This phrase is repeated in the prefaces to the other five volumes included in *Eighteen Discourses.*

# BIBLIOGRAPHICAL NOTE

For general bibliographies of Kierkegaard studies, see:

Jens Himmelstrup, *Søren Kierkegaard International Bibliografi.* Copenhagen: Nyt Nordisk Forlag Arnold Busck, 1962.
Aage Jørgensen, *Søren Kierkegaard-litteratur 1961–1970.* Aarhus: Akademisk Boghandel, 1971. *Søren Kierkegaard-litteratur 1971–1980.* Aarhus: privately published, 1983. *"Søren Kierkegaard-litteratur 1981–1990. Udkast til bibliografi,"* Uriasposten, VIII, 1989.
Bruce H. Kirmmse, *Kierkegaard in Golden Age Denmark.* Bloomington: Indiana University Press, 1990.
François H. Lapointe, *Sören Kierkegaard and His Critics: An International Bibliography of Criticism.* Westport, Connecticut: Greenwood Press, 1980.
*International Kierkegaard Newsletter,* ed. Julia Watkin. Copenhagen: 1979–.
*Kierkegaard: A Collection of Critical Essays,* ed. Josiah Thompson. New York: Doubleday (Anchor Books), 1972.
*Kierkegaardiana,* XII, 1982; XIII, 1984; XIV, 1988.
*Søren Kierkegaard's Journals and Papers,* I, ed. and tr. Howard V. Hong and Edna H. Hong, assisted by Gregor Malantschuk. Bloomington: Indiana University Press, 1967.

For topical bibliographies of Kierkegaard studies, see *Søren Kierkegaard's Journals and Papers,* I-IV, 1967–75.

# INDEX

scholarship: and pastor, 123–24;
theological, 122–26; and upbuilding discourses, 111
seeking: and change, 23, 27; God, 9,
15, 17–28, 132–33; and loss, 23,
27; and road, 20; and striving,
19–20; what is given, 23, 27–28;
and wish, 17–19; and wonder,
18–23
self: conception of, 52, 58, 60–63,
67–68; concern about, 117; denial
of, 114–15; and resolution, 52,
58, 60–63, 67–68; understanding
of, 139
self-esteem: diminishing, 29
sensuality: and death, 83
servant: and recollection, 77
Shakespeare, William: *The Complete
Works*, 165; *Hamlet*, 164–65;
*Twelfth Night*, 112
sickness: and death, 12, 74
sigh: and worship, 16
silence: and death, 86
sin(s), sinner: and comparison, 30–
32; confession and, 32; discourse
and, 28, 35; God and, 15, 28–32,
130, 133; greatest, 30–31, 136;
and marriage, 139; particular, 32,
34; and purity, 119; single individual as, 29–32; and sorrow, 29–
30, 113; and wedding, 57; woman
who was, 35; and worship, 117
single individual: discourse and, x,
120–21; and earnestness, 76; and
the essential, 38; reader as, x, 129;
as sinner, 29–32
sleep: death as, 80–82, 145
Socrates, 124–25, 161; and daimon,
161; and Xanthippe, 115
Solon: and Croesus, 165–66
sorrow: and death, 74; and God,
130; and sin, 29–30, 113
soul: darkness in, 137
speaker, speaking, 119; and authority, x, 44–45; Christian art of,

viii–ix, 110–11; good, 120; and
listener, 102, 120; and reader, x,
127
speculation: and theology, 122
spy (spies): authority and, 136
stillness: and change, 36–37; and
conceit, 14–15; in confession, 9–
17; and conscience, 11; discourse
on, 15–17; and fear, 11, 14; and
forgiveness, 13–14; and God, 39–
40; and guilt, 14, 38–39; obtain-
ment of, 11; as transition, 12
striving: and seeking, 19–20; and
wonder, 20
suffering, 150; and comfort, 115;
and comparison, 30; and death,
81–82; as guilty, ix, 115–16

teacher: death as, 102
thanksgiving: for happiness, 63–65;
and resolution, 64–65
theology: and scholarship, 122–26;
and speculation, 122
Thiers, Adolphe, *Den franske Revolutions Historie*, 168
thought: of death, 75–85, 89–102,
143
time: and death, 83–85, 96; and
eternity, 44; and life, 78; merchant and, 83–84; scarcity of, 83–
85; as test, 49; and wisdom, 33
transformation: death as, 99. *See
also* change
transition, 12, 111, 150. *See also*
change
tree: axe at root of, 93
truth: and opinion, 99–100

uncertainty: and death, 94–96, 99–
102, 150–52
understanding: of self, 139; and
wonder, 26
unknown, the: and wonder, 18–21
upbringing: as presupposition, 21–
22

upbuilding: and choice, 120. *See also*
discourse(s), upbuilding

venturing, 134

way: is narrow, 32
wedding: in Cana, 62; and choice,
44–45; as covenant for eternity,
43–45; and distinction, 46–47;
and earnestness, 45–46; and freedom, 43; and resolution, 47–48,
50, 52–53, 57; and sin, 57
Winther, Christian, *Sagn og Sang*,
127
wisdom: and time, 33
wish, wishing: and change, 33; and
seeking, 17–19; and wonder, 17–
19, 22–23
woman: Canaanite, ix, 115; "*In
Vino Veritas*" on, xiii; who was
sinner, 35

wonder: and blessedness, 24; and despair, 22–23; discourse and, 22–
23; and fear, 24–26; ocean and, 19;
and seeking, 18–23; and striving,
20; true, 135; and understanding,
26; and the unknown, 18–21; and
wish, 17–19, 22–23; and worship,
18–20; youth and, 18, 22
work, working: and death, 96
world: renunciation of, 14
worship: and sigh, 16; as sinner,
117; and wonder, 18–20

Xanthippe: and death of Socrates,
115
Xenophon: *Memorabilia*, 160, 161;
*Opera*, 160

youth, 20, 135; and death, 94, 101–
02; and old age, 21; and wonder,
18, 22

# ADVISORY BOARD

## KIERKEGAARD'S WRITINGS